This Book is provided with the sole purpose of providing relevant information on a specific topic for which every reasonable effort has been made to ensure that it is both accurate and reasonable. Nevertheless, by purchasing this Book you consent to the fact that the author, as well as the publisher, are in no way experts on the topics contained herein, regardless of any claims as such that may be made within. It is recommended that you always consult a professional prior to undertaking any of the advice or techniques discussed within.This is a legally binding declaration that is considered both valid and fair by both the Committee of Publishers Association and the American Bar Association and should be considered as legally binding within the United States.

CONTENTS

Introduction

Every person has a different journey in diabetes. However, the one thing that can be the same for everyone is enjoying life and doing the things you love doing.

Diabetes is a chronic disease, which has become widespread in the modern age. One of the reasons behind this is our sedentary lifestyle and poor dietary habits.

Since we spend most of our time at our workplaces and stay busy throughout the day, we do not have time to make healthy meals, even if it's for ourselves. Due to this, we gorge on fast foods and processed foods. This drastically affects our health and has made ailments like diabetes permanent.

And, people who try to eat healthy, first search the internet for tasty and healthy recipes. But, not every website can provide the right information about the meals you can cook in type 2 diabetes. There is a lot of misleading information on the internet that can further worsen your diabetes.

This is why I decided to write down this cookbook that incorporates delectable and easy to cook meals for people suffering from type 2 diabetes.

Plus, the focal point of these meals is that all of them can be cooked in a crock pot. These recipes will help you live a healthier, longer, and fun life with type 2 diabetes.

Even if someone else in your family has type 2 diabetes, you can make these recipes for them and they will surely love them. This cookbook includes 300 simple to make crock pot recipes for diabetics.

The recipes won't take a lot of time, which makes them ideal for today's busy people who don't have much time to cook food. These recipes are for breakfast, lunch, dinner, snacks, and dessert.

Moreover, by making these meals in your crock pot, you can eat delicious, nourishing, cost-effective, and diabetic-friendly dishes. A crock pot saves your time as it can cook in your absence and is easy to operate. Plus, it takes up little space owing to its compact size and is simple to clean. You can make these satisfying, nutritious, and wholesome recipes in a few minutes every day.

Which foods are good for health and which foods to avoid in type 2 diabetes?

If you have type 2 diabetes, you would already be aware that this condition has no cure. But, you can manage it with the right attention and care. This includes changing your lifestyle, constantly checking your blood sugar, and regularly doing exercise. And, primarily, you must change your poor dietary habits with healthy meals.

People who have type 2 diabetes can consume meals with different ratios of carbohydrates, fats, and proteins. Among these, the major sources of fats and proteins should be plants and that of carbohydrates should be low glycemic foods, such as vegetables, fruits, low-fat milk, and whole grains.

You can consume healthy fats, irrespective of you being a diabetic or not. One of the healthy fats includes monounsaturated fat, which is found in canola oil, extra-virgin olive oil, avocado, nuts, sesame seeds, peanut butter and oil, etc.

Plus, one other healthy fat is polyunsaturated fat. This is found in plant-based oil, salad dressings, walnuts, sunflower oil, soft margarine, mayonnaise, etc.

Omega-3 fatty acids are also good for diabetics. They are found in fish like herring, mackerel, salmon, albacore tuna, sardines, anchovies, rainbow trout, etc.

Fruits and vegetables are great for diabetics as they have lots of fiber, vitamins, and minerals with low calories. You can have them as you like, frozen, canned, fresh, or dried.

Your diet should include different fruits so that you can get as many vitamins and minerals as possible. Nevertheless, make sure you avoid fruit juices and smoothies as they have zero fiber.

Starchy foods are also good for people with diabetes. Starch is present in rice, potatoes, naan, chapattis, pasta, plantain, etc. However, some starchy foods, called high glycemic index foods, can increase the blood glucose levels, which is why they should be avoided. Rather, you can eat foods with low glycemic levels, including brown rice, wild rice, whole grains, etc.

Apart from these, you should eat leafy greens, eggs, cinnamon, chia seeds, natural unprocessed greek yogurt, turmeric, different types of nuts excluding peanuts, flaxseeds, strawberries, apple cider vinegar, squash, garlic, and avocado.

You should avoid foods with unhealthy fats, including cholesterol and trans-fat. Trans-fat is present in stick margarine, processed foods, and fast foods. And, cholesterol is present in high-fat dairy items, egg yolk, poultry skin, and high-fat meat.

Plus, you must avoid sugar-sweetened beverages, flavored milk, and iced teas as they have a high carb and fructose content, which can result in insulin resistance. White rice, white pasta, and white bread should also be avoided since they are high in carbohydrates and low in fiber and nutrients.

You must also avoid fruit-flavored yogurt, processed dairy products, sweetened breakfast cereals, honey, maple syrup, agave nectar, white sugar, packaged processed snacks, and fried foods like french fries.

What is a crock pot?

Crack pot is a common electrical kitchen appliance that is useful in the winter and fall. It is also known as a slow cooker as both these appliances are quite similar.

The term 'crock pot' came into existence following a trademark owned by Sunbeam Products. The main difference between a crock pot and a slow cooker is that as mentioned before a crock pot is a slow cooker brand, which popularized a type of slow cooker. But, all slow cookers are not crack pots.

This cooking appliance can be placed on the kitchen counter and used for simmering foods at low temperatures. This temperature is lower than other conventional cooking methods, like frying, boiling, and baking. Since a crock pot works on low temperatures, you don't have to constantly check on the food and you can safely leave it for long time periods.

A crock pot is small in size and made of three main parts, including a heating element, a glass lid, and a porcelain or ceramic pot. The pot is situated within the heating unit and is oval or round in shape. It is offered in several sizes.

A crock pot uses moist heat in order to cook food continuously for several hours or as per the set timer. Most of these appliances are heated from the sides and base.

Crock pots have two heat settings, wherein the high heat setting is of around 300 degrees Fahrenheit and the low heat setting is of around 200 degrees Fahrenheit. A few crock pots come with a third heat setting as well, which is a lower, warmer heat setting.

You can cook a wide array of recipes in a crock pot, including recipes for type 2 diabetes. It is great for making pot roasts, sauces, stews, soups, beverages, dips, snacks, and desserts. You can also make bread and cocoa in a crock pot, foods that are usually made quickly. A crock pot can also be used to make the hard meat tender.

Benefits of using a crock pot

There are several advantages of using a crock pot. The main benefits of a crock pot include:

- Crock pots are easy and convenient to use.
- Using a crock pot is a healthy cooking method, which promotes good health. This is because it works at low temperatures, which leads to the lowest amount of nutrient loss.
- Foods cooked in crock pots have rich flavors since they are cooked for several hours.
- A crock pot uses very little power as compared to traditional cooking processes; equal to a fraction of a standard stove or oven. This reduces your power bills and energy costs, thus saving your money.
- While cooking in a crock pot, you don't have to continuously check or monitor the food as compared to conventional cooking processes. This also saves your time. All you need to do is put the food inside the crock pot, switch it on, set the desired time and temperature, and you are done. You can start the crock pot when you leave your home and when you return, your food will be prepared. How cool and convenient is that!
- Since the food is cooked on a low temperature inside a crock pot, you don't have to worry about it getting burnt, stuck, scorched, or overcooked.
- Meat is tenderized with the extended cooking process of a crock pot, which saves your money in costly meat cuts and provides tastier results.
- Crock pots are easy to clean since you just have to take out the cooking pot or liner and clean it. Moreover, the low temperature and glazed pot make it easier to wash as compared to traditional high-heat pots. The food is cooked in only one pot, which further reduces the wastage of water that arises from washing numerous dishes.

Crock pot usage tips and safety

A crock pot is a convenient kitchen appliance to make a delicious meal with minimum effort. You just have to put all the ingredients in it, switch it on, go to your office, and when you come home, your dinner will be all set for you to eat.

Apart from this, you can also make overnight oatmeal, stews, dips, etc. in a crock pot. However, while using a crock pot, you must know some usage and safety rules in order to make your cooking process easier and safe. Some of the common crock pot usage tips are:

- When you purchase a crock pot, make sure you read all the instructions mentioned in its user manual. You will find that a crock pot is quite simple to operate.
- In order to prepare the food, you just need to cut the vegetables and put them inside the crock pot. Then, you have to switch it on and set the timer and temperature.
- When putting in the food inside the crock pot, make sure you put the root or dense vegetables at the pot's bottom, close to the heat source, since they take more time to cook. Then, if you're using meat, you can put it after the vegetables at the second number. After this, you can add spices and herbs to the container. Finally, you must add a sufficient amount of water because if there is not enough water, the food can dry out and will not be cooked properly in the crock pot, which uses moisture and low heat to cook food. Plus, ensure that the pot is filled around one-third to three-fourth.
- Some seafood and dairy items can burn quickly and get spoiled, it is best to add them in the final cooking hour.
- Make sure you properly cover the container with its lid since a tight lid can ensure minimum evaporation.
- While the food is cooking, don't lift the lid to check on the food since this will further extend the cooking time by 30 minutes due to the heat loss.

Crock pot cooking times

A crock pot has its cooking time guidelines in its instruction manual that comes with it. Generally, the cooking time conversion for a crock pot is:

- When the regular cooking time is 15 to 30 minutes, then the crock pot will take 1 to 2 hours on high heat setting and 4 to 6 hours on low heat setting to cook the food.
- When the regular cooking time is 30 minutes to 1 hour, then the crock pot will take 2 to 3 hours on high heat setting and 5 to 7 hours on low heat setting to cook the food.
- When the regular cooking time is 1 to 2 hours, then the crock pot will take 3 to 4 hours on high heat setting and 6 to 8 hours on low heat setting to cook the food.
- When the regular cooking time is 2 to 4 hours, then the crock pot will take 4 to 6 hours on high heat setting and 8 to 12 hours on low heat setting to cook the food.

Breakfast & Brunch

Shrimp & Broccoli Breakfast Casserole

Servings: 10
Cooking Time: 2 ½ Hours
Ingredients:
- nonstick cooking spray
- 2 cups broccoli florets
- 12 eggs
- 1 cup skim milk
- 1 cup onion, diced
- 2 cups cheddar cheese, grated
- ¼ cup green onion, diced
- 2 cloves garlic, diced fine
- 1 green bell pepper, chopped
- ¼ cup sundried tomatoes, diced
- 1 lb. shrimp, peeled & deveined

Directions:
1. spray crock pot with cooking spray.
2. Place broccoli in an even layer in the pot.
3. In a large bowl, whisk together eggs and milk until combined.
4. stir in remaining ingredients. Pour over broccoli, making sure the egg mixture is even.
5. Cover and cook on high 2-2 ½ hours, or on low 4-4 ½ hours. the casserole is done when the eggs are set. serve immediately.

Nutrition Facts:Per Serving: Calories 328, total Carbs 19g, net Carbs 7g, Fiber , Protein 31g, Fat 19g, saturated Fat 9g, sugar 4g, sodium 414mg, Cholesterol 406mg

Cool Breakfast Burritos

Servings: 2
Cooking Time: 7 Hours
Ingredients:
- 4 fresh Eggs
- ½ a cup of diced Red Potatoes
- ¼ of a cup of milk, Dairy or Nut
- ¼ of a cup of diced Ham
- ¼ of a Green Capsicum, finely diced
- 1 tsp of dried Basil
- Sea Salt and freshly cracked Black Pepper to taste
- 1 tbsp of Olive Oil

Directions:
1. Oil your slow cooker liner with a little oil and place the potatoes inside, add the diced capsicum and ham, then sprinkle with the dried basil
2. Place the lid on top and cook for 6 to 8 hours on low
3. Serve by placing a spoonful of the egg and potato mixture into a pita or flat bread

Nutrition Facts:Per Serving:358 cal, 2g total fat, 5.3g sat fat, 340mg chol, 573mg sodium, 16.4g carb, 3.4g fiber, 19,9 Protein

Amazing Overnight Apple And Cinnamon Oatmeal

Servings:2
Cooking Time: 7 Hours
Ingredients:
- ¾ cup coconut milk
- 1 diced whole apple
- ½ cup steel cut oats
- ½ tbsp raw honey
- 1 tbsp coconut oil
- ¾ cup water, fresh
- ¼ tbsp salt to taste, sea
- 1 tbsp cinnamon

Directions:
1. Spray your crockpot with cooking oil. This is to prevent food from sticking.
2. Add water, coconut milk, apples, oats, coconut oil, raw honey, salt, and cinnamon. Stir to combine.
3. Cover and cook for about 6-7 hours on low.
4. Serve hot with favorite toppings.

Nutrition Facts:Per Serving: Calories: 284, total fat: 17.9g, saturated fat: 1, total carbs: 30.3g, net carbs: 25.6g, protein: 4.2g, sugars: 1.3g, fiber: 4.7g, sodium: 30mg, potassium: 90mg

Mouth Watering Egg Casserole

Servings: 2
Cooking Time: 10 Hours
Ingredients:
- 1oz of Prosciutto or Ham, cut into ½ inch slices
- ½ a cup of Button Mushrooms, thinly sliced
- 1 tbsp of Red Capsicum, seeded and thinly sliced
- ¼ of a cup of cooked diced Potatoes
- ¼ of a cup of frozen and chopped Spinach, thawed and drained
- ¼ of a cup of frozen Artichoke Hearts, thawed, then quartered
- 1 tbsp of Sun-dried Tomatoes, drained and then chopped up
- 1oz of Swiss Cheese, diced
- 1oz of Goat Feta Cheese
- 2 fresh Eggs
- 1 tsp of Dijon Mustard
- 1 cup of Whole Milk
- Sea Salt and freshly Cracked Black pepper to Taste
- A few fresh whole Basil Leaves for garnish

Directions:
1. Place a crockpot liner inside your 2 quart slow cooker and give it a coating of cooking oil
2. Grill the prosciutto until it becomes crisp, about 4 minutes, retain the fat
3. Sauté the capsicum and mushrooms until soft, about 4 minutes in the butter and fat
4. Place the potatoes in the base of your crockpot and on top, place half of the capsicum mushroom mixture in an even layer
5. Add half the artichoke hearts, the spinach and the sundried tomatoes in layers
6. Sprinkle on half the Swiss cheese, follow this with the remaining vegetables in layers and the remaining cheese then the feta cheese
7. Combine together the milk, eggs and mustard and pour this mixture over the vegetables to settle through the whole dish
8. Place the crisped prosciutto on top
9. Cook the bake for 8 hours on low or for 4 hours on high. Remove the casserole from the crockpot using the liner. Then rest it for about 10 minutes before removing the liner
10. Slice and serve it with the fresh basil leaves as a garnish and serve with a leafy green salad

Nutrition Facts:Per Serving:297 cal, 17g total fat, sat. fat, 212mg chol, 416mg Sodium, 20.8g carb, 2.4g fiber, 15.8g Protein

Dreamy Lemon Berry Steel Cut Oats

Servings:2
Cooking Time: 5-8 Hours
Ingredients:
- 1 cup steel-cut oats
- 1 tbsp pomegranate molasses
- 1 tbsp grated lemon zest
- 1 tbsp lemon juice
- 1 cup fresh strawberries and cranberries
- 1 tbsp olive oil
- 4 cups water
- ½ cup coconut milk
- ½ tbsp salt
- ¼ cup chia seeds

Directions:
1. Preheat your crockpot.
2. Meanwhile, sauté oil and oats, then toast in the crockpot, while stirring constantly.
3. Add water, milk, and molasses to the pot and mix together.
4. Add lemon zest, lemon juice, and salt, then stir to mix well.
5. Cover and cook for about 8 hours on low.
6. Add chia seeds and berries then mix well.
7. Allow the mixture to rest for a few minutes and serve with cow's cream.

Nutrition Facts:Per Serving: Calories: 420, total fat: 17.5g, saturated fat: 3.3g, total carbs: 35.2g, net carbs: 24.6g, protein: 14.9g, sugars: 1.95g, fiber: 10.6g, sodium: 372mg, potassium: 161mg

Delicious Apple Blueberry Risotto

Servings: 2
Cooking Time: 8 Hours
Ingredients:
- 2 tbsp of Olive Oil
- 1 cup of Arborio rice
- 2 large Fresh Apples, cored, diced
- 1 cup of Apple juice
- 1 cup of dried Blueberries
- 1 tsp of ground Cinnamon
- 1 tsp of Sea Salt
- 2 cups of Nut or Dairy Milk

Directions:
1. Place the oil in your cooker bowl and using the sauté option, cook the rice until heated and has a nice golden color (If your crockpot does not have a sauté option, use a separate pan)
2. Cook the rice on high for 4 to 5 hours or low for 7 to 8 hours
3. Once the rice is cooked, add the blueberries and mix them well together
4. Serve this dish at room temperature
5. Garnish the dish with sliced nuts and or fresh fruit.

Nutrition Facts:Per Serving:825 cal, 23.3g total fat, 7g sat. fat, 24mg chol, 424mg Sodium, 142.8g carb, 10.6g fiber, 15.5g Protein

Delectable Potato Bake

Servings: 2
Cooking Time: 8 Hours
Ingredients:

- ½lb of Potatoes, diced into 1/2in cubes
- 2oz of Canadian Bacon
- 1 diced Onion
- ½ a cup of Cheddar Cheese, shredded
- 3 tbsp of grated Parmesan
- 4 fresh Eggs
- ¼ of a cup of Fresh Milk
- 1 tbsp of Flour
- Sea Salt and White Pepper to taste

Directions:

1. Lightly oil the inside of your crockpot and layer one third of the diced potatoes on the bottom. Then place a layer of bacon, a layer of onion and a layer of cheese on top
2. Repeat with another layer each of potatoes, bacon, onion and cheese
3. Then place the final layer of potatoes, bacon, onion and cheese
4. Whisk the rest of the ingredients in a bowl and pouring them over the mixture in your crockpot
5. Place on the lid and cook for 6 to 8 hours on low

Nutrition Facts:Per Serving:cal 9, total fat,40.7g, sat fat 22.6, chol 436mg, sodium 1305mg, carb 28.9g, fiber 3.9g, protein 48.8g

Wonderful Spicy Breakfast Casserole

Servings:2
Cooking Time: 8 Hours
Ingredients:

- 2 whole apples, medium and thinly sliced
- 1 cup natural muesli
- ½ tbsp Cinnamon
- 1 tbsp butter, Unsalted

Directions:

1. Place the apples in a crockpot then add all the remaining ingredients.
2. Cover the pot and cook for about 8 hours.
3. Remove and serve with pure dairy cream.

Nutrition Facts:Per Serving: Calories: 218, total fat: 7g, saturated fat: 2g, total carbs: 38g, net carbs: 3, protein: 3g, sugars: 9.5g, fiber: 4g, sodium: 15mg, potassium: 181mg

Flavorful Greek Egg Casserole

Servings: 2
Cooking Time: 4 Hours
Ingredients:
- 4 fresh Eggs, whisked together
- 1 cups of Baby Spinach, sliced
- 1 cup of finely sliced Button Mushrooms
- 1 small finely diced Red Onion
- ¼ of a cup of Sun-dried Tomatoes
- 1 tbsp of Nut or Dairy
- ¼ of a cup of Feta Cheese
- 1 tsp of Garlic Powder
- Freshly ground Black Pepper to taste
- Sea Salt to taste

Directions:
1. Place the eggs, milk, garlic powder, salt & pepper in a bowl and whisk them together
2. Add the onion, mushrooms and sun-dried tomatoes
3. Pour this mixture into your slow cooker and add the feta cheese
4. Place on the lid and cook on low for to 6 hours

Nutrition Facts:Per Serving:2 cal, 15.6g total fat, 5.3g sat fat, 496 chol, 536mg. 10g carb, 1.4g fiber, 20.2g protein

Cauliflower Oatmeal

Servings:1
Cooking Time: 10 Minutes
Ingredients:
- 1 cup cauliflower rice
- ½ cup almond milk, unsweetened
- 1 sliced strawberry
- ¼ tbsp stevia
- ½ tbsp cinnamon
- ½ tbsp peanut butter

Directions:
1. Place the rice in a crockpot then add milk, stevia, and cinnamon. Boil over high heat while stirring.
2. Reduce heat to low and continue to boil for about 8-10 minutes while stirring.
3. Add more milk if too thick and transfer to a bowl.
4. Drizzle the cauliflower oatmeal with peanut butter then top with strawberry slices.
5. Serve and enjoy.

Nutrition Facts:Per Serving: Calories: 139, total fat: 6g, saturated fat: 0.8g, total carbs: 16.3g, net carbs: 9g, protein: 6.8g, sugars: 5.8g, fiber: 7.3g, sodium: 230.3g, potassium: 217.3mg

Crockpot Breakfast Casserole

Servings:8
Cooking Time: 6 Hours
Ingredients:

- 16-ounce frozen potatoes, hash brown
- ½ pound bacon, cooked and diced
- ½ cup diced mushrooms
- 2 cups milk
- 2 cups cheddar cheese, shredded
- ½ cup onion, chopped
- 10 eggs, large
- Pepper to taste
- Salt to taste

Directions:

1. Place potatoes, cheese, onion, bacon, and mushrooms in a bowl. Stir together.
2. Add pepper and salt, then place in a crockpot. Make sure the crockpot is prepared by spraying cooking oil.
3. Whisk eggs and milk together then pour over mixture in the crockpot — season with pepper and salt.
4. Cover the crockpot and cook for about 6-7 hours. Ensure the eggs are set.
5. Serve and enjoy.

Nutrition Facts:Per Serving: Calories: 419 total fat: 28g saturated fat: 12.3g total carbs: 13.9g net carbs: 12.3g protein: 27. sugars: 4.4g fiber: 1.6g sodium: 959mg potassium: 552mg

Apple Pecan Breakfast Pudding

Servings: 6
Cooking Time: 4 Hours
Ingredients:

- nonstick cooking spray
- 12 slices whole-wheat baguette, 1-inch thick
- 4 eggs
- ¾ cup almond milk
- 1 tbsp. stevia
- 2 tbsp. maple syrup
- 1 tbsp. vanilla
- 1 tsp cinnamon
- 1 large apple, peeled & diced
- ½ lemon, freshly squeezed
- ½ cup pecans, chopped

Directions:

1. spray the crock pot with cooking spray.
2. Place the bread sliced in an even layer on the bottom of the pot.
3. In a large bowl, whisk together eggs, milk, stevia, syrup, vanilla, and cinnamon. Pour over bread, making sure each slice is completely covered.
4. In a separate mixing bowl, combine apples and lemon juice and toss to coat. Place apples on top of the ingredients in the pot. sprinkle pecans over the top.
5. Cover and cook on low 4 hours, or on high 2 hours until the bread pudding passes the toothpick test. serve warm.

Nutrition Facts:Per Serving: Calories 292, total Carbs 39g, net Carbs 3, Fiber 3g, Protein 10g, Fat 10g, saturated Fat 2g, sugar 12g, sodium 365mg, Cholesterol 107mg

Tantalizing Cranberry Apple French Toast

Servings:2
Cooking Time: 5 Hours
Ingredients:
- 1 loaf of Yesterday's French Bread
- 1 large whole Apple, cut to bite size chunks
- 4 fresh Eggs
- 1/4 of a cup of dried Cranberries (or any berries)
- ¾ of a cup of Cashew or Almond Nut Milk
- ½ a cup of Coconut Cream or full Cream Milk
- 1 tbsp of Pomegranate Molasses
- 1 tbsp of Raw Honey
- 1/2 tbsp of Vanilla Extract
- ¼ of a tbsp of Cinnamon or Nutmeg

Directions:
1. Slice the bread into n cubes
2. Lightly oil your crockpot bowl
3. Place the apple, cranberries and bread in the crockpot and mix together
4. Whisk together the milks, eggs, honey, vanilla, pomegranate molasses and cinnamon. Then pour the egg mixture over the mixture in your crockpot and stir to mix evenly
5. Place on the lid and cook the French bread for to 6 hours on low

Nutrition Facts:Per Serving:402 cal, 15.1g total fat, 4.9g sat fat, 281 chol, 22g sodium, 4.9 fiber, 14.4 Protein

Tomato & Mozzarella Crustless Quiche

Servings: 8
Cooking Time: 4 Hours
Ingredients:
- nonstick cooking spray
- 6 eggs
- 1 cup mozzarella cheese, grated, divided
- ½ tsp baking soda
- ¼ cup skim milk
- 2 tbsp. fresh thyme, chopped fine
- ¼ tsp salt
- ¼ tsp black pepper
- 2 medium tomatoes, chopped
- 1 yellow bell pepper, chopped

Directions:
1. spray crock pot with cooking spray.
2. In a large bowl, whisk together eggs, mozzarella, baking soda, milk, thyme, salt, and pepper.
3. stir in tomatoes and bell pepper and toss to combine. Pour into the crock pot.
4. Add the lid and cook on high 2 ½ hours, or on low hours, quiche is done when the eggs are set. serve immediately.

Nutrition Facts:Per Serving: Calories 97, total Carbs 3g, net Carbs 2g, Fiber 1g, Protein 9g, Fat , saturated Fat 2g, sugar 2g, sodium 300mg, Cholesterol 143mg

Apple & Pumpkin Oatmeal

Servings: 4
Cooking Time: 6 Hours
Ingredients:
- 1 ½ cups water
- ½ cup apple juice, sugar-free
- ½ cup pumpkin puree
- ½ cup apples, chopped fine
- 1 ¼ cups steel cut oats
- ½ tsp cinnamon
- ¼ tsp nutmeg

Directions:
1. Place all ingredients in crock pot and stir to combine.
2. Add the lid and cook on low heat for 6 hours, or high heat for 3 hours, stirring occasionally.
3. stir well before serving.

Nutrition Facts:Per Serving: Calories 223, total Carbs g, net Carbs 34g, Fiber 7g, Protein 9g, Fat 3g, saturated Fat 1g, sugar 5g, sodium 4mg, Cholesterol 0mg

Savory Oatmeal

Servings: 4
Cooking Time: 6 Hours
Ingredients:
- 3 cups chicken broth, low sodium
- ½ cup skim milk
- 1 cup steel-cut oats
- ½ tsp salt
- ¼ cup cheddar cheese, grated
- 2 tbsp. Parmesan cheese, grated
- 6 slices turkey bacon, cooked crisp & crumbled
- 2 tbsp. chives, diced

Directions:
1. Add the broth, milk, oats, and salt to the crock pot.
2. Add the lid and cook on low heat 5 hours, stirring occasionally
3. stir in the cheddar and Parmesan cheese and cook another 60 minutes.
4. Ladle oatmeal into bowls and top with bacon and chives. serve immediately.

Nutrition Facts:Per Serving: Calories 3, total Carbs 18g, net Carbs 16g, Fiber 2g, Protein 17g, Fat 24g, saturated Fat 9g, sugar 3g, sodium 674mg, Cholesterol 41mg

Berry French Toast Casserole

Servings: 8
Cooking Time: 3 Hours
Ingredients:

- Butter flavored cooking spray
- 2 cups whole grain bread, cubed
- 4 egg whites
- 1 cup coconut milk
- 2 tbsp. maple syrup
- 1 tsp vanilla
- ½ tsp almond extract
- 1 tsp ground cinnamon
- 1 cup blueberries

Directions:

1. spray the crock pot with cooking spray.
2. Place the bread in an even layer on the bottom of the pot.
3. In a large bowl, whisk together egg whites, milk, syrup, vanilla, almond extract, and cinnamon.
4. Pour egg mixture over bread and stir to coat well. sprinkle blueberries over the top.
5. Add the lid and cook on low 6 hours, or high for 3 hours. the casserole is done when it passes the toothpick test. serve immediately.

Nutrition Facts:Per Serving: Calories 123, total Carbs 13g, net Carbs 10g, Fiber 3g, Protein 4g, Fat 7g, saturated Fat 5g, sugar , sodium 76mg, Cholesterol 0mg

Mouth-watering Egg Casserole

Servings:2
Cooking Time: 10 Hours
Ingredients:

- 10oz ham, ½ -inch slices
- ½ cup thinly sliced button mushrooms
- 1 tbsp seeded red capsicum, thinly sliced
- ¼ cup thawed artichoke hearts, frozen and quartered
- Whole basil leaves, fresh
- ¼ cup diced potatoes, cooked
- 1 tbsp drained tomatoes, sun-dried and chopped up
- ¼ cup thawed and drained spinach, chopped and frozen
- 10oz diced Swiss cheese
- 10oz goat feta cheese
- 2 eggs
- 1 cup whole milk
- 1 tbsp Dijon mustard
- Sea salt to taste
- Black pepper freshly cracked to taste

Directions:

1. Place a coated crockpot liner with cooking oil inside a crockpot, 2-qt
2. Grill the ham pieces for about 4 minutes until crisp. Retain the fat.
3. Sauté mushrooms and capsicum in the fat and butter for about 4 minutes until soft.
4. Place potatoes in the crockpot base and on top, then place an even layer of mushroom-capsicum mixture.
5. Add half of artichokes, tomatoes, and spinach in layers then sprinkle with half swiss cheese, followed by remaining vegetables, then remaining cheese and feta cheese.
6. Meanwhile, combine eggs, milk, and mustard in a bowl then pour over to settle through on the dish.
7. Place ham on top.
8. Cover and cook for about hours on low then use the liner to remove the casserole.
9. Rest for about 10 minutes, then remove the liner.
10. Slice the casserole and garnish with basil leaves.
11. Serve alongside with green salad, leafy.

Nutrition Facts:Per Serving: Calories: 297, total fat: 17g, saturated fat: 11g, total carbs: 20.8g, net carbs: 18.4g, protein: 15.8g, sugars: 10.2g, fiber: 2.4g, sodium: 416mg, potassium: 617mg

Peanut Butter & Banana Oatmeal Bars

Servings: 8
Cooking Time: 4 Hours
Ingredients:
- Butter flavored cooking spray
- 1 ½ cups rolled oats
- 1/3 cup stevia
- 1 tsp baking powder
- ¾ cup almond milk
- 2 tbsp. coconut oil, melted
- 1 egg
- ½ cup peanut butter, sugar-free
- 1 tsp vanilla
- 1 banana, sliced

Directions:
1. spray the crock pot with cooking spray.
2. In a large bowl, combine oats, stevia, and baking powder.
3. stir in milk, oil, egg, peanut butter, and vanilla until thoroughly combined.
4. Press mixture, in an even layer, in the crock pot. Lay the sliced bananas over the top.
5. Add the lid and cook on low heat 6 hours, or high heat 3 hours, until edges start to brown. Let cool 10 minutes before slicing and serving.

Nutrition Facts:Per Serving: Calories 295, total Carbs 35g, net Carbs 30g, Fiber 5g, Protein 9g, Fat 15g, saturated Fat 5g, sugar 11g, sodium 7g, Cholesterol 20mg

Bacon & Tomato Grits

Servings: 4
Cooking Time: 3 Hours
Ingredients:
- 1 cup green bell pepper, diced
- ¼ cup water
- 1 cup grape tomatoes, quartered
- ½ cup green onion, diced
- ¼ tsp thyme
- 2 tsp hot sauce
- 1/3 cup quick-cooking grits
- 8 slices turkey bacon, center-cut
- 1 oz. sharp cheddar cheese, grated

Directions:
1. Add peppers, water, tomatoes, onion, thyme and hot sauce to the crock pot, stir to mix.
2. Add cover and cook on high 3 hours or until peppers are still tender-crisp.
3. Cook grits according to package directions.
4. Cook bacon in a large skillet over med-high heat until crisp. drain on a paper towel-lined plate.
5. When pepper mixture is done, ladle grits into bowls and top with peppers. sprinkle with crumbled bacon and cheese and serve.

Nutrition Facts:Per Serving: Calories 89, total Carbs 8g, net Carbs 7g, Fiber 1g, Protein 5g, Fat 5g, saturated Fat 1g, sugar 2g, sodium 347mg, Cholesterol 20mg

Poultry Recipes

Super Tasty Tex-mex Chicken

Servings: 2
Cooking Time: 6 Hours
Ingredients:
- 1/2lb of boneless, Skinless Chicken Thighs
- ½ a cup of frozen Onion and Pepper strips, thawed
- ½ a cup of frozen Yellow Corn
- 1/4 of a cup of Water
- ½ a cup of diced Tomatoes and Green Chilies
- ½ a tsp of ground Cumin
- ½ a tsp of Tex-Mex Seasoning

Directions:
1. Sauté the chicken so its browned on both sides and place it in your crockpot
2. Then sauté the onions and peppers until just tender
3. Place the onions and peppers with the chicken and add the water and tomatoes.
4. Cook covered on low for hours and stir in the cumin
5. Cook them for an additional 30 minutes, or until thighs become very tender
6. Serve

Nutrition Facts:Per Serving: Cal 138, total fat 8.3g, sat fat 2g, Chol 48mg, sodium 114mg, Carb 6.4g, fiber 1.2g, protein 10.6g

Chicken Mushroom Stew

Servings:6
Cooking Time: 5 Hours 45 Minutes
Ingredients:
- 6 chicken breast halves, boneless and skinless
- 8 oz fresh sliced mushroom
- 3 cups zucchini, diced
- 1 cup green pepper, chopped
- 2 tbsp divided canola oil
- 1 diced medium onion
- 4 minced garlic cloves
- 3 chopped medium tomatoes
- 6 oz tomato paste
- ¾ cup water
- 2 tbsp each dried basil
- 2 tbsp thyme
- 2 tbsp marjoram
- 2 tbsp oregano

Directions:
1. Cut the chicken into small cubes and place it in a skillet.
2. Brown the chicken with one tablespoon oil and transfer into a crockpot.
3. Using the same skillet sauté, the mushroom, onion, zucchini, and green pepper in remaining oil until they become tender-crisp then transfer the mixture to the crockpot.
4. Add garlic to the crockpot and cook for one minute.
5. Transfer the mixture into the crockpot and add tomatoes, tomato paste, water, basil, thyme, marjoram, and oregano.
6. cover and cook for five hours
7. Serve and enjoy.

Nutrition Facts:Per Serving: Calories 237, Total Fat , Saturated Fat 1g, Total Carbs 15g, Net Carbs 12g, Protein 27g, Sugar 7g, Fiber 3g, Sodium 82mg

Caribbean Curried Chicken

Servings:8
Cooking Time: 6 Hours 15 Minutes
Ingredients:

- 1 tbsp madras curry powder
- 4 oz chicken thigh boneless and skinless
- 1 sliced medium onion
- 1 ½ cups Goya mojo Criollo marinade
- 1 tbsp garlic powder
- 1 tbsp pepper
- 1 tbsp canola oil
- 2 tbsp all-purpose flour
- Green onions for serving
- Cilantro leaves for serving

Directions:

1. Mix madras curry powder, garlic powder, and pepper in a bowl and sprinkle it over chicken as you press so that it can adhere properly.
2. Put the chicken in a crockpot and sprinkle onions on it.
3. Pour mojo criollo marinade on the sides of the crockpot avoiding contact with the chicken.
4. Cover and cook for six hours.
5. Remove the chicken from heat and put it in a hot dish.
6. Put cooking juice from the crockpot in a cup and skim fat.
7. In a saucepan, pour oil and heat it as you whisk in flour until smooth.
8. Pour the cooking juices into the mixture.
9. Stir cook the mixture and allow it to boil for two minutes so that the mixture thickens.
10. Add the chicken into the mixture and simmer for five minutes.
11. Serve with rice, green onions, and cilantro and enjoy.

Nutrition Facts:Per Serving: Calories 249, Total Fat 13g, Saturated Fat 3g, Total Carbs 11g, Net Carbs 10g, Protein 22g, Sugar 5g, Fiber 1g, Sodium 514mg

Lovely Chicken With Oranges, And Yellow Capsicum

Servings: 2
Cooking Time: 7 Hours
Ingredients:

- 4 Chicken Drum Sticks
- 1 Orange, peeled and sliced into rings
- 1 small Yellow sliced Capsicum
- ½ a cup of Tomato Salsa or crushed Tomatoes with Basil
- ½ a cup of Chicken Stock
- 1 small, Medium, Hot Chili, deseeded and sliced
- 1 small, thinly sliced Onion
- 1 clove of minced Garlic
- 1 cup of Quinoa
- Sea Salt and Black Pepper to taste
- ¼ a cup of chopped fresh Cilantro Leaves

Directions:

1. Place the quinoa in your crockpot with the chicken drumsticks
2. Pour the stock and salsa over the chicken
3. Add the capsicum, garlic, chili and onion
4. Place the orange rings on top of the chicken
5. Cook covered on low for 7 hours
6. Serve with the fresh cilantro leaves

Nutrition Facts:Per Serving: Cal 4, total fat 25.6g, sat fat 6.7g, chol 180mg, sodium 354mg, carb 76.7g fiber 10.8g, protein 53.5g

Turkey In Cream Sauce

Servings:8
Cooking Time: 8 Hours 15 Minutes
Ingredients:
- 1 ¼ cups white wine
- 2 bay leaves
- 2 tbsp crushed and dried rosemary
- ¾ lb turkey breast tenderloins each
- ½ cup whole or cream
- 1 chopped medium onion
- 2 minced garlic cloves
- ½ tbsp pepper
- 3 tbsp cornstarch
- ½ tbsp salt

Directions:
1. Add wine, onion, garlic, and bay leaves in a crockpot.
2. Mix rosemary and pepper in a bowl, then rub over the turkey and put them in the crockpot.
3. Cover the crockpot and cook for eight hours.
4. When time is done, remove the turkey and put it in a serving platter
5. Skim fat from cooking juice, put the juice in a saucepan and heat to boil.
6. In the hot liquid stir in cornstarch, cream, and salt and allow it boil it for two minutes.
7. Serve with turkey and enjoy it.

Nutrition Facts:Per Serving: Calories 205, Total Fat 3g, Saturated Fat 1g, Total Carbs 6g, Net Carbs 5g, Protein 32g, Sugar 1g, Fiber 0g, Sodium 231mg

Chicken Satay

Servings: 4
Cooking Time: 4 Hours
Ingredients:
- 1 tbsp. olive oil
- 6 chicken tenders, boneless & skinless
- 1 stalk lemongrass, chopped
- 1/3 cup coconut milk, unsweetened
- 2 tbsp. fish sauce
- 1 tbsp. fresh lime juice
- 1 tbsp. lite soy sauce
- 1 tsp sriracha sauce
- 1 tsp stevia
- 1 tsp ginger
- 1 tsp turmeric
- 2 cloves garlic, diced fine

Directions:
1. Heat oil in a large skillet over med-high heat.
2. Add chicken and cook until browned on the outside. transfer to the crock pot.
3. In a medium bowl, stir together remaining ingredients and pour over chicken.
4. Add the lid and cook on low heat 3-hours, or on high 2-3 hours until chicken is cooked through.

Nutrition Facts:Per Serving: Calories 37 total Carbs 8g, net Carbs 7g, Fiber 1g, Protein 25g, Fat 25g, saturated Fat 10g, sugar 4g, sodium 927mg, Cholesterol 96mg

Moroccan Chicken With Apricots, Olives And Almonds

Servings: 2
Cooking Time: 4 Hours
Ingredients:
- 1lbs of skinless Chicken Thighs
- 1 small Onion, cut into 1/2-inch wedges
- 1 tsp of Ground Cumin
- 1/2 a tsp of Ground Ginger
- 1/2 a tsp of Ground Coriander
- ¼ of a tsp of Ground Cinnamon
- 1/4 of a tsp of Cayenne Pepper
- 1 Bay Leaf
- 1/3 of a cup of low-sodium Chicken Stock or Broth
- ½ a cup of drained and rinsed Chickpeas
- 1/2 a cup of Green Olives
- ¼ of a cup of dried Apricots
- ¼ of a cup of Sliced Almonds
- Sea Salt and ground Black Pepper to taste

Directions:
1. Place the chicken with the onion, cumin, ginger, coriander, cinnamon and cayenne in a bowl and season with salt and pepper before mixing well
2. Place the chicken and onion mixture in your crockpot
3. Add the bay leaf and cook, covered, on high for 2 hours
4. Stir in the chickpeas, olives, and apricots, then cook for another two hours or until the apricots have become plump and the chicken is tender
5. Adjust the seasoning if necessary and remove the bay leaf
6. Toast the almonds until they are golden and fragrant
7. Place the chicken and accompanying juices in 2 bowls, sprinkle them with almonds and serve with Couscous

Nutrition Facts:Per Serving:6 cal, 30g total fat, 7.4g sat fat, 389mg sodium, 34.8g carb, 10g fiber, 109.4g protein

Chicken With Artichokes & Red Peppers

Servings: 8
Cooking Time: 8 Hours
Ingredients:
- 12 oz. jar roasted red peppers, drain & chop
- ¾ cup chicken broth, low sodium
- 4 whole chicken breasts
- 3 cloves garlic, diced fine
- 1/4 sweet onion, diced fine
- 1 tsp salt
- ½ tsp pepper
- 4 tbsp. cream cheese, fat-free
- 4 tbsp. Parmesan cheese, grated
- 14 oz. artichoke hearts, drain & chop
- 1 cup cherry tomatoes, chopped

Directions:
1. Add red peppers, broth, and chicken to the crock pot.
2. sprinkle garlic, onion, salt, and pepper over the top.
3. Add the lid and cook on low heat 6-8 hours or on high 4-6 hours.
4. transfer chicken to serving plates.
5. Add the cream cheese, parmesan, and artichokes to the crock pot. stir until cheese has melted and sauce is creamy. spoon over chicken, top with tomatoes and serve.

Nutrition Facts:Per Serving: Calories 239, total Carbs 12g, net Carbs 8g, Fiber 4g, Protein 25g, Fat 10g, saturated Fat 4g, sugar 4g, sodium 584mg, Cholesterol mg

Curried Chicken & Peppers

Servings: 6
Cooking Time: 2 ½ Hours
Ingredients:
- 1 red bell pepper, cut in 1/2-inch strips
- 1 yellow bell pepper, cut in 1/2-inch strips
- 1 onion, cut in thin wedges
- ¼ cup golden raisins
- 3 cloves garlic, diced fine
- 3 lbs.chicken thighs, boneless & skinless
- 14 ½ oz. diced tomatoes, undrained
- 2 tsp curry powder
- 1 tsp cumin
- 2 tbsp. flour

Directions:
1. Place the peppers, onion, raisins, garlic, and chicken in the crock pot.
2. In a mixing bowl, combine tomatoes, seasonings, and flour until mixed well. Pour over chicken.
3. Add the lid and cook on high 2 ½ - hours, or on low 5-6 hours until chicken is cooked through and tender.

Nutrition Facts:Per Serving: Calories 521, total Carbs 17g, net Carbs 15g, Fiber 2g, Protein 65g, Fat21 g, saturated Fat 5g, sugar 7g, sodium 16mg, Cholesterol 293mg

Amazing Spicy Chicken

Servings:2
Cooking Time:7 Hours
Ingredients:
- ½lbs of Chicken Breasts or Boneless Chicken Thighs
- 1 cup of cooked Quinoa
- 1 tbsp of Tamari sauce or Coconut Aminos
- 1/4 of a cup of Rice Wine Vinegar or Apple Cider Vinegar
- 1 tbsp of Mirin or dry Sherry
- 1 tsp of Toasted Sesame Oil
- 2 cloves of minced Garlic
- 1 tsp of minced Ginger
- 1/8 of a tsp of Red Chili Flakes (optional)
- Sea Salt and freshly ground Black Pepper, to taste
- 1 tbsp of Corn Starch
- 1 tbsp of fresh Water
- For garnish: sliced green onions, sesame seeds

Directions:
1. First season the chicken liberally with sea salt and pepper, then sear it on a hot grill or pan
2. Place the breasts in your slow cooker bowl
3. Whisk together the sesame oil, tamari sauce, mirin, vinegar, ginger and garlic, then pour this mixture over the chicken
4. Cook it covered on low for 6 to 7 hours or high for 3 to hours
5. Once the chicken is tender, mix the cornstarch with water and stir it in to form the sauce
6. Serve on top of the quinoa or if preferred rice

Nutrition Facts:Per Serving:65 cal, total fat 6g, sat fat 2 g, 124 chol, 12mg sodium, 53g carb, 1g fiber, 44g protein

Cheesy Chicken Broccoli Casserole

Servings: 2
Cooking Time: 4 Hours
Ingredients:
- 1/2lb of Chicken Breast, chopped into 1 inch pieces
- ½ a cup of Raw Broccoli Florets
- 1 cup uncooked Brown Rice
- 1/2 of a diced Red Onion
- 1 tbsp of minced Garlic
- 1 tsp of Thyme
- 1 tsp of Rosemary
- 2 cups of Chicken Stock or Broth
- ½ a cup of Greek Yogurt
- 2/3 of a cup of mixed cheeses such as Monterey Jack, Parmesan, Cheddar
- 1 tbsp of Olive Oil
- Sea Salt and freshly ground Black Pepper to taste

Directions:
1. Sauté the garlic and onion for a few minutes in the olive oil
2. Add the uncooked rice, the fresh rosemary and fresh thyme
3. Then add the diced chicken and stock
4. Cook covered on high for 3 to 5 hours
5. About an hour before serving the chicken, add the yogurt and cheeses, stirring well to combine completely
6. Place the raw broccoli florets straight on top of the rice without stirring them in, allowing them to cook in the steam and remain crunchy

Nutrition Facts:Per Serving:0 cal, fat 27.2g, sat fat 10.4g chol 116mg, sodium 1093mg, 52.1g protein, 82.2g carb, 5g fiber

Lovely Roasted Red Capsicum Chicken

Servings: 2
Cooking Time: 4 Hours
Ingredients:
- 2 medium Chicken Breasts
- 1 medium diced Onion
- 2 cloves of minced Garlic
- ½ a cup of roughly chopped Roasted, Red Capsicum
- ½ a cup of Kalamata Olives
- 1 tbsp of Capers
- 1 tbsp of fresh Lemon Juice
- 2 tsp of Italian Seasoning
- Sea Salt and freshly ground Black Pepper to taste
- Olive Oil as Needed
- Fresh herbs like Basil or Thyme to Garnish

Directions:
1. Use salt and pepper to season the chicken before sauté it for 2 minutes on each side
2. Transfer the chicken to your well-oiled crockpot
3. Add the red peppers, onions, olives and capers to your slow cooker around and on the sides of the chicken
4. Mix together the Italian seasoning, lemon juice and garlic and spread this over the chicken
5. Cook covered on low for 4 hours or on high for 2 hours. Garnish with fresh thyme or oregano, then serve hot

Nutrition Facts:Per Serving:cal 325, total fat.13g, sat fat 13g, chol 128mg, sodium 113mg, carb 8.5g, fiber 1.8g, protein 41.7g

Turkey Breast With Gravy

Servings:12
Cooking Time: 6 Hours 15 Minutes
Ingredients:

- 2 tbsp parsley, dried and in flakes
- 1 tbsp poultry seasoning
- 3 medium carrots
- 3 chopped celery ribs
- 6 lb bone-in and skinless turkey breast
- 1tbsp salt
- ½ tbsp paprika
- ½ tbsp pepper
- 2 chopped medium onions
- ½ cup all-purpose flour
- ½ cup water

Directions:

1. Mix parsley, salt, poultry seasoning, paprika and pepper in a bowl
2. Put the onions, carrots, and celery in a crockpot and place the turkey on top.
3. Rub the turkey with the seasoning mixture in the bowl.
4. Cover and cook for six hours.
5. Remove turkey from the crockpot and put it on a chopping board and slice it after fifteen minutes.
6. Put cooking juices into a saucepan.
7. In another bowl, mix flour and water until they become smooth then stir in the mixture into the cooking juices.
8. Heat the mixture as you stir and allow it to boil for two minutes.
9. Serve with the turkey and enjoy it.

Nutrition Facts:Per Serving: Calories 200, Total Fat 1g, Saturated Fat 0g, Total Carbs 2g, Net Carbs 2g, Protein 43g, Sugar 0g, Fiber 0g, Sodium 270mg

Italian Chicken With Sweet Potatoes

Servings: 4
Cooking Time: 6 Hours
Ingredients:

- 4 chicken breasts, boneless & skinless
- 8 oz. cremini mushrooms, halved
- 2 cups sweet potatoes, chopped
- ¼ cup fresh lemon juice
- ½ cup chicken broth, low sodium
- ¼ cup extra-virgin olive oil
- 1 tsp oregano
- 1 tsp parsley
- 1 tsp basil
- 1 tsp salt
- ½ tsp black pepper
- ½ tsp onion powder
- 2 cloves garlic, diced fine

Directions:

1. Place the chicken in the middle of the crock pot.
2. Place potatoes on one side, and mushrooms on the other side of the chicken.
3. In a medium bowl, whisk together the remaining ingredients and pour over chicken and vegetables.
4. Add the lid and cook on low heat 6 hours, or on high 3-4 hours until chicken is cooked through and potatoes are tender.

Nutrition Facts:Per Serving: Calories 364, total Carbs 33g, net Carbs 28g, Fiber , Protein 24g, Fat 16g, saturated Fat 2g, sugar 8g, sodium 700mg, Cholesterol 62mg

Teriyaki Chicken & "rice"

Servings: 6
Cooking Time: 4 Hours
Ingredients:
- 2 tbsp. cornstarch
- ½ cup + 2 tbsp. water
- ¾ cup soy sauce, low sodium
- ¼ cup stevia brown sugar
- ½ tsp ginger
- ½ tsp garlic, diced fine
- 12 oz. bag stir fry vegetables
- 3 cups cauliflower, grated
- 2 chicken breasts, boneless & skinless

Directions:
1. In a measuring cup, stir together cornstarch and 2 tablespoons water until smooth.
2. In a small saucepan, combine soy sauce, ½ cup water, stevia, ginger, and garlic. Cover and bring to a boil over medium heat.
3. Remove lid and stir in cornstarch mixture. Cook until the sauce starts to thicken, about 1 minute.
4. spray the crock pot with cooking spray. Place the vegetables on the bottom of the crock pot.
5. Lay the chicken on top of the vegetables and pour the sauce over the top.
6. Add the lid and cook on low heat 4 hours, or until chicken is tender.
7. Remove the chicken and using 2 forks shred it. Return the chicken back to the crock pot and stir everything together. serve.

Nutrition Facts:Per Serving: Calories 143, total Carbs 1, net Carbs 16g, Fiber 2g, Protein 22g, Fat 2g, saturated Fat 0g, sugar 2g, sodium 1208mg, Cholesterol 57mg

Chicken & Zucchini Stew

Servings: 6
Cooking Time: 4 Hours
Ingredients:
- 2 tbsp. olive oil
- 6 chicken breasts, boneless, skinless & cut in 1-inch pieces
- 8 oz. mushrooms, sliced
- 1 onion, chopped
- 3 cups zucchini, chopped
- 1 cup green bell pepper, chopped
- 4 cloves garlic, diced fine
- 3 tomatoes, chopped
- 6 oz. tomato paste
- ¾ cup water
- 2 tsp thyme
- 2 tsp oregano
- 2 tsp marjoram
- 2 tsp basil

Directions:
1. Heat oil in a large skillet over med-high heat. Add chicken and cook until lightly browned. transfer the chicken to the crock pot.
2. Add the mushrooms, onion, zucchini, and bell pepper to the skillet and cook 3-5 minutes, or until vegetables start to soften.
3. Add the garlic and cook 1 minute more.
4. Add the vegetables to the chicken with the remaining ingredients stir to combine.
5. Add the lid and cook on low heat 4-hours or until chicken is cooked through.

Nutrition Facts:Per Serving: Calories 383, total Carbs 13g, net Carbs 10g, Fiber 3g, Protein 57g, Fat 11g, saturated Fat 2g, sugar 7g, sodium 130mg, Cholesterol 172mg

Greek Lemon Chicken

Servings: 4
Cooking Time: 4 Hours
Ingredients:
- 4 chicken breast, boneless & skinless
- 4 cloves garlic, diced fine
- 1 tsp salt
- 3 tsp oregano
- ¼ cup fresh lemon juice
- 1 tbsp. lemon zest
- 1 cup chicken broth, low sodium
- 3 tbsp. fresh parsley, chopped

Directions:
1. Place the chicken in the crock pot. Add remaining ingredients, except parsley, over the chicken.
2. Add the lid and cook on low heat 6 hours, or on high for 4 hours until chicken is cooked through.
3. serve hot garnished with parsley.

Nutrition Facts:Per Serving: Calories 237, total Carbs 5g, net Carbs , Fiber 1g, Protein 40g, Fat 5g, saturated Fat 1g, sugar 1g, sodium 589mg, Cholesterol 125mg

Polynesian Chicken

Servings: 6
Cooking Time: 6 Hours
Ingredients:
- 20 oz. pineapple chunks, in natural juice
- 1 tbsp. soy sauce, low sodium
- 1 clove garlic, diced fine
- 1 tsp fresh ginger, grated
- 1/3 cup honey
- 1 tbsp. cornstarch
- 4 chicken breasts, boneless, skinless, cut in 1-inch pieces
- 8 oz. can water chestnuts, drain & slice
- 1 red bell pepper, cut in 1-inch strips

Directions:
1. In a small bowl, whisk together juice from the pineapple, soy sauce, garlic, ginger, and honey until combined.
2. Add cornstarch and mix well.
3. Place chicken in the crock pot and pour the sauce over. Add the lid and cook on low heat 4-6 hours, or until chicken is cooked through.
4. Add the bell pepper, chestnuts, and pineapple during the last 30 minutes of cooking time. serve immediately.

Nutrition Facts:Per Serving: Calories 2, total Carbs 31g, net Carbs 29g, Fiber 2g, Protein 18g, Fat 7g, saturated Fat 2g, sugar 16g, sodium 468mg, Cholesterol 24mg

Tender Crockpot Duck

Servings: 2
Cooking Time:7 Hours
Ingredients:
- 1 whole Duck
- 2 medium whole Carrots
- 1 medium Onion
- 2 sticks of Celery
- 4 small whole potatoes
- 2 sprigs of fresh Rosemary
- 1 small bunch of fresh Thyme
- 1 medium whole Orange
- 1 large piece of Cheesecloth (to help lift the duck from your crockpot)

Directions:
1. Remove the duck giblets and remove any visible fat, then wash it in clean fresh water
2. Dry the duck and rub it inside and out with salt and pepper
3. Quarter the onion and orange and place them inside the duck with the sprigs of thyme and rosemary
4. Use the sauté option or a fry pan to brown the outside of the duck
5. Place the vegetables in such a way as to make a stand at the bottom of your crockpot to keep the duck above the liquid
6. Place the duck on the cheesecloth and prick the skin several times to allow any fat to escape, then tie the cheesecloth to encase the bird and make a handle to lift it out when cooked
7. Cook covered on low for hours or high for 4 hours. About half way through cooking, check that the fat (liquid) level is below the duck, if not remove it using a syringe or spoon
8. When cooked, remove the duck from your crockpot, remove the cheese cloth and allow it to sit for 10 minutes before slicing

Nutrition Facts:Per Serving: Cal 281, total fat 14.1g, sat fat 4.7g, chol 27mg, sodium 38mg, carb31., fiber 7.4g, protein 7.2g

Tomato Balsamic Crockpot Chicken

Servings:6
Cooking Time: 7 Hours

Ingredients:

- 2 chopped medium carrots
- 2lb chicken thighs, bone-in and skinless
- ½ cup chicken broth, reduced-sodium
- 1 bay leaf
- Orzo, hot cooked
- ½ cup shallot, sliced
- 1tbsp flour, all-purpose
- 14½ oz tomatoes, diced and undrained
- ¼ cup vinegar, balsamic
- 1tbsp olive oil
- 2 minced garlic cloves
- ½ tbsp Italian seasoning
- ½ tbsp salt
- ¼ tbsp pepper

Directions:

1. Put carrots and shallots in a crockpot and place the chicken on top.
2. Whisk flour and broth in a bowl until smooth, then stir in tomatoes, vinegar, oil, garlic, bay leaf, and seasoning.
3. Pour the mixture in the bowl over the chicken, cover, and cook for seven hours.
4. When time is done, remove the chicken and place it on a chopping board and discard bay leaf
5. Remove the bones from chicken bones and return it to the crockpot then heat through.
6. Serve with orzo and enjoy

Nutrition Facts:Per Serving: Calories 235, Total Fat 11g, Saturated Fat 3g, Total Carbs 12g, Net Carbs 10g, Protein 23g, Sugar , Fiber 2g, Sodium 433mg

Balsamic Chicken

Servings: 10
Cooking Time: 4 Hours

Ingredients:

- 1 tbsp. olive oil
- 6 chicken breasts, boneless & skinless
- salt & pepper, to taste
- 1 onion, sliced thin
- 1 tsp oregano
- 1 tsp basil
- 1 tsp rosemary
- ½ tsp thyme
- 4 cloves garlic
- ½ cup balsamic vinegar
- 2 (14 ½ oz) can tomatoes, diced

Directions:

1. Pour the oil in the crock pot and add the chicken.
2. sprinkle salt and pepper over each piece of chicken.
3. top chicken with onion, herbs, and garlic.
4. Pour vinegar over the top then add tomatoes, undrained.
5. Add the lid and cook on high 4 hours, or until chicken is cooked through.
6. Remove chicken and slice, serve over pasta topped with sauce.

Nutrition Facts:Per Serving: Calories 238, total Carbs , net Carbs 5g, Fiber 2g, Protein 25g, Fat 12g, saturated Fat 3g, sugar 4g, sodium 170mg, Cholesterol 73mg

Alluring Turkey With Mushroom Sauce

Servings: 2
Cooking Time: 7 Hours
Ingredients:
- 1 small (1lb) turkey breast
- 1 tbsp of Unsalted Butter
- 1 tbsp of Dried Parsley Flakes
- ½ a tsp of Dried Tarragon Flakes
- ½ a tsp of Sea Salt
- ¼ of a tsp of Freshly Ground Black Pepper
- ¼ of a cup of Chicken Broth
- ¼ of a cup of Dry White Wine
- 1 cup of finely sliced Fresh Mushrooms
- 1 tbsp of Cornstarch

Directions:
1. Place the turkey in your crockpot and brush it with the butter
2. Sprinkle the mushrooms, tarragon, parsley, salt and pepper over it and pour the wine and stock around it
3. Cook covered on low for 8 hours
4. Remove the turkey and slice it into 2 portions.
5. Skim off any excess fat and turn the crockpot to high setting
6. Combine the cornstarch with a little water and add it to the juices and mushrooms in the crockpot, stirring constantly until thickened then serve over or beside the turkey

Nutrition Facts:Per Serving: Cal 308, Fat 14g Sat fat 5g, carbs 3g, Protein 38g, Chol 118mg, Sodium 32g, Calcium 31mg

Southern Fried Chicken

Servings: 2
Cooking Time: 2 ½ Hours
Ingredients:
- nonstick cooking spray
- 2 chicken breast, boneless & skinless
- ½ cup buttermilk, reduced fat
- ½ cup white whole wheat flour
- ¼ tsp black pepper
- ¼ tsp smoked paprika
- ¼ tsp garlic powder
- ¼ tsp salt
- ½ cup whole-wheat panko bread crumbs

Directions:
1. spray the crock pot with cooking spray.
2. Add the buttermilk to a small bowl.
3. In a separate bowl, combine flour and seasonings.
4. Place the bread crumbs in a shallow dish.
5. dip each chicken in the buttermilk, dredge in flour mixture, then dip in buttermilk again.
6. Press the chicken into the bread crumbs to thoroughly coat both sides. Place in the crock pot.
7. Add the lid and cook on high 2 ½ hours or until chicken is cooked through. Remove the lid and cook another 10 minutes to crisp the chicken. serve.

Nutrition Facts:Per Serving: Calories 379, total Carbs 36g, net Carbs 32g, Fiber 4g, Protein 31g, Fat 12g, saturated Fat 3g, sugar 4g, sodium 446mg, Cholesterol 73mg

Chicken And Mushroom Supreme

Servings:2
Cooking Time: 4 Hours

Ingredients:

- ½ a cup of Whole Grain Flour
- 1lb of Broiler Chicken into bite sized pieces
- 1 tsp of Coconut or Olive Oil
- 1 medium Onion, sliced into wedges
- 1 small sliced Capsicum
- 1 cup of finely sliced Fresh Mushrooms
- 1 clove of minced Garlic
- ½ a cup of Diced Tomatoes
- ½ a cup of Chicken Stock
- ½ a tsp of Dried Oregano
- ½ a tsp of Dried Basil
- Sea Salt and Black Pepper to taste
- ¼ of a cup of Shredded Parmesan Cheese

Directions:

1. Place the flour and ¼ of a tsp of salt and pepper in a plastic bag, then add a few pieces of the chicken at a time and shake to coat them evenly
2. Sauté the chicken in your crockpot or a heavy pan to brown. Then place them in your crockpot
3. Add the onions, capsicum, mushrooms, tomatoes, garlic, chicken stock, oregano and basil and cook covered for 5 hours or the chicken and vegetables are tender
4. Serve the chicken garnished with Parmesan cheese

Nutrition Facts:Per Serving: Cal 277, Fat 11g, Sat fat 3g, Carbs 1, protein 29g, fiber 2g, Chol 85mg, Sodium 463mg, Calcium 146mg

Mediterranean Turkey Patties

Servings: 2
Cooking Time: 8 Hours
Ingredients:
- ¼ of a cup of Greek yogurt
- 1 tbsp of fresh Lemon Juice
- ½ a tbsp of fresh Lime Juice
- 2 cloves of Garlic, finely chopped
- ¼ of a tsp of dried Dill
- ½lb of ground Turkey
- 1 small Red Onion, thinly sliced
- 1 small Red Onion, finely chopped
- 1 tbsp of finely chopped sun-dried tomatoes
- 2oz of frozen Spinach, thawed out, chopped and drained
- 6 tbsp of crumbled Feta Cheese
- 1 tsp of dried Oregano
- ½ cup of Whole Grain Breadcrumbs
- 1 large egg
- Sea salt and ground black pepper to taste; optional
- 1 small, cooked Beet, sliced thinly
- ¼ of a medium sized Cucumber, sliced thinly

Directions:
1. First prepare the yogurt sauce, combine the lemon juice, yogurt ½ the garlic clove with the dill in a small bowl. Mix them well and place the sauce in your refrigerator, covered, until needed
2. Mix together the, chopped onion, spinach, sun-dried tomatoes, 1/clove of garlic, cheese, oregano, egg, turkey, bread crumbs, salt and pepper
3. Using clean wet hands, form the mixture into six even sized patties about 1 inch thick
4. Place the patties in your crockpot bowl, leaving a space between them
5. Cook them covered on low for 6 to 8 hours
6. They can be served with a bun or with couscous and the yogurt sauce

Nutrition Facts:Per Serving:258 cal, 13g total fat, 5g sat fat, 286 mg sodium, 125 chol, 8g carb, 1g fiber, 28g protein

Chicken Cacciatore

Servings: 6
Cooking Time: 4 Hours
Ingredients:
- ⅓ cup flour
- 3-4 lbs. chicken, skinless & cut in pieces
- 2 tbsp. olive oil
- 2 onions, cut in wedges
- 1 green bell pepper, cut in strips
- 6 oz. mushrooms, sliced
- 14 oz. tomatoes, diced, undrained
- 2 cloves garlic, diced fine
- 1/8 tsp salt
- ½ tsp oregano
- ¼ tsp basil
- ½ cup Parmesan cheese, grated

Directions:
1. Place flour in a large plastic bag. Add chicken, a few pieces at a time, and shake to coat.
2. Heat oil in a large skillet over medium heat. Add chicken and brown on both sides. transfer chicken to the crock pot.
3. Place the onions, bell pepper, and mushrooms over the chicken.
4. In a small bowl, combine tomatoes, garlic, and seasonings. Pour over the vegetables.
5. Add the lid and cook on low heat 4-hours or until chicken is cooked through and vegetables are tender.
6. transfer to a serving plate and garnish with parmesan cheese before serving.

Nutrition Facts:Per Serving: Calories 4, total Carbs 15g, net Carbs 13g, Fiber 2g, Protein 67g, Fat 15g, saturated Fat 4g, sugar 4g, sodium 436mg, Cholesterol 204mg

Greek Chicken Stew

Servings: 8
Cooking Time: 6 Hours
Ingredients:
- 3 tbsp. extra virgin olive oil
- 8 chicken thighs, boneless
- 1 tsp salt
- 1 tsp pepper
- 1 tbsp. Greek seasoning
- 1 cup onion, chopped
- 2 tbsp. fresh lemon juice
- 2 tsp fresh oregano, chopped
- 4 cloves garlic, peeled
- 2 tbsp. garlic, diced fine
- 1 cup chicken broth, low sodium
- 1 cup Kalamata olives, pitted
- ½ cup roasted red pepper, chopped
- 1 tbsp. capers, drained
- ¼ cup sundried tomatoes, chopped
- 4 cups cauliflower, grated

Directions:
1. Heat oil in a large skillet over med-high heat.
2. sprinkle chicken with salt, pepper, and Greek seasoning.
3. Cook in the skillet until brown on both sides. transfer to the crock pot.
4. Add onion, lemon juice, and oregano to the skillet and cook until onion begins to soften.
5. Add garlic and cook 1 minute more. Add to chicken.
6. Add the remaining ingredients and stir to mix.
7. Add the lid and cook on low heat 5-6 hours, or until chicken is cooked through.

Nutrition Facts:Per Serving: Calories 470, total Carbs , net Carbs 5g, Fiber 3g, Protein 52g, Fat 25g, saturated Fat 5g, sugar 3g, sodium 619mg, Cholesterol 49mg

Chicken & Wild Rice Soup

Servings: 8
Cooking Time: 6 Hours
Ingredients:
- 1 cup wild rice, uncooked
- 3 chicken breasts, boneless & skinless
- 1 cup onion, diced small
- ½ cup carrot, peeled & diced small
- ½ cup celery, peeled & diced small
- 6 cups chicken broth, low sodium
- ½ tsp sage
- ¼ tsp thyme
- ¼ tsp rosemary
- ½ tsp salt
- ½ tsp black pepper
- 2 cups plain Greek yogurt
- ¼ cup fresh parsley, chopped

Directions:
1. Rinse the rice and place it in the crock pot.
2. Add chicken, vegetables, broth, and seasonings, stir to mix.
3. Add the lid and cook on high 4 hours, or on low 6-8 hours, until chicken is cooked through and tender.
4. Remove chicken to a bowl and shred. Return it to the crock pot along with the yogurt. stir until smooth. (If you like a thicker consistency, mix equal parts cornstarch and water and stir into soup. Cook until soup reaches desired consistency). serve garnished with parsley.

Nutrition Facts:Per Serving: Calories 2, total Carbs 22g, net Carbs 20g, Fiber 2g, Protein 26g, Fat 7g, saturated Fat 3g, sugar 4g, sodium 246mg, Cholesterol 56mg

Chicken Enchiladas

Servings: 6
Cooking Time: 4 Hours
Ingredients:
- 2 chicken breast, boneless
- 1 tsp cumin
- 1 tsp chili powder
- ½ tsp garlic powder
- ½ tsp black pepper
- 4 oz. jalapenos, diced
- 16 oz. jarred enchilada sauce, sugar-free
- 1 cup sour cream, fat-free, divided
- 1 ½ cups cheddar cheese, grated
- 6 medium whole-grain tortillas

Directions:
1. Heat oven to 350 °F.
2. Place chicken in a baking dish and cover. Bake 35-45 minutes or until cooked through.
3. Remove skin from the chicken and shred with 2 forks.
4. In a medium bowl, add chicken and seasonings and mix to coat.
5. stir in jalapenos, ½ cup enchilada sauce, ½ cup sour cream, and 1 cup cheese and mix well.
6. Place ½ cup of mixture in the middle of each tortilla and roll up.
7. Place 3 enchiladas on the bottom of the crock pot and top with some of the sauce. Repeat with remaining enchiladas and sauce.
8. In a small bowl, whisk together remaining enchilada sauce and ½ cup sour cream. Pour over enchiladas. Add lid and cook on low heat 3-4 hours or until bubbly.
9. Carefully remove enchiladas, one at a time, and transfer to a serving plate. top with sauce and sprinkle cheese over. serve immediately.

Nutrition Facts:Per Serving: Calories 294, total Carbs 29g, net Carbs 26g, Fiber 3g, Protein 16g, Fat 13g, saturated Fat 6g, sugar 3g, sodium 422mg, Cholesterol 45mg

Turkey With Berry Compote

Servings:12
Cooking Time:4 Hours 20 Minutes
Ingredients:
- ½ tbsp thyme, dried
- ½ tbsp pepper
- 2 cups raspberries
- 2 cups blueberries
- 1 cup grape juice, white
- 1 tbsp salt
- ½ tbsp garlic powder
- ½ tbsp pepper
- ⅓ Cup water
- 2 peeled and chopped medium apples
- ¼ tbsp red pepper, crushed and in flakes
- ¼ tbsp ginger, ground

Directions:
1. In a bowl, mix salt, garlic powder, thyme, and pepper and rub the turkey with the mixture
2. Put the turkey on a crockpot and pour water on the turkey.
3. Cover and cook for four hours.
4. When time elapses, remove the turkey from crockpot and put it on a chopping board.
5. Cover the turkey with foil and allow it to rest for ten minutes, then slice it.
6. Combine apples, raspberries, blueberries, grape juice red pepper, and ginger in a saucepan.
7. Cook the compote ingredients as you stir until the mixture thickens, and the apple become tender for twenty minutes.
8. Serve with turkey and enjoy it.

Nutrition Facts:Per Serving: Calories 215, Total Fat 1g, Saturated Fat 0g, Total Carbs 12g, Net Carbs 10g, Protein 38g, Sugar 8g, Fiber 2g, Sodium 272mg

Turkey Sausage & Barley Soup

Servings: 6
Cooking Time: 5 Hours
Ingredients:
- 1 lb. turkey sausage
- 1 onion, chopped
- 1 cup carrot, peel & dice
- ½ cup pearl barley
- 3 ½ cups chicken broth, low sodium
- 1 tsp salt
- ½ tsp black pepper
- 2 (15 oz) cans petite diced tomatoes
- 1 tbsp. tomato paste
- 3 cups kale, chopped

Directions:
1. Heat a skillet over medium heat. Add the sausage and cook, breaking up with a spatula, until no longer pink. drain off fat and transfer sausage to the crock pot.
2. Add onion, carrot, barley, broth, salt, pepper, and tomatoes. stir to mix.
3. Add the lid and cook on low heat 4 – 4/12 hours or until barley is tender.
4. stir in the tomato paste and kale. Cover and cook another 30 minutes until the kale has wilted. serve immediately.

Nutrition Facts:Per Serving: Calories 279 total Carbs 29g, net Carbs 21g, Fiber 8g, Protein 23g, Fat 9g, saturated Fat 2g, sugar 9g, sodium 704mg, Cholesterol 61mg

Delicious Chicken, Corn And Bean Chili

Servings:2
Cooking Time: 6 Hours
Ingredients:
- ½lb of cubed Chicken breasts
- ½ a cup of chopped Onion
- 1 tbsp of Coconut or Olive Oil
- ¼ of a cup of rinsed Cannellini Beans
- 1/2 a cup of Diced Tomatoes liquid included
- 1 tbsp of mild Green Chilies
- ¼ of a cup of Frozen Yellow Corn
- 1 tsp of minced Garlic
- ¼ of a tsp of Ground Cumin
- ¼ tsp celery salt
- ¼ tsp of Ground Coriander
- Sea Salt and Black Pepper to taste
- Sour Cream and Shredded Cheddar for serving

Directions:
1. Sauté the chicken and onions in your crockpot or a fry pan
2. Add the beans, corn, tomatoes and spices
3. Cook covered on low for 5 hours or until the chicken is tender
4. Serve with sour cream and cheese

Nutrition Facts:Per Serving: Cal 304, Fat 10g, Sat fat 1g, Carbs 22g, Protein 30g, Fiber , Chol 75mg, Sodium 455mg, Calcium 66mg

Chicken & Squash Stew

Servings: 4
Cooking Time: 4 Hours
Ingredients:
- 2 tbsp. extra virgin olive oil
- ¼ cup flour
- 1 lb. chicken breasts, cut in bite-sized pieces
- ½ tsp salt
- 1/8 tsp pepper
- 2 ½ cups chicken broth, low sodium
- 1 onion, chopped
- 2 squash, diced
- 3 fresh sage leaves, chopped

Directions:
1. Heat 1/2 tablespoons oil in a large skillet over medium heat.
2. Place flour in a large Ziploc bag. Add chicken and toss to coat.
3. Add the chicken to the skillet and cook until brown on the outside. season with salt and pepper.
4. Add 1 cup broth and continue cooking until the sauce begins to thicken.
5. transfer the chicken and sauce to the crock pot.
6. Add remaining oil to the skillet along with the onion. Cook about 5 minutes or until onion turns translucent. Add to the crock pot.
7. Add remaining ingredients and stir to mix.
8. Add the lid and cook on low heat 4 hours. stir before serving.

Nutrition Facts:Per Serving: Calories 2, total Carbs 21g, net Carbs 17g, Fiber 4g, Protein 27g, Fat 12g, saturated Fat 2g, sugar 5g, sodium 245mg, Cholesterol 69mg

Tender Chicken With Zucchini Noodles And Basil Pesto

Servings: 2
Cooking Time: 8 Hours

Ingredients:
- 6oz of Chicken Breasts, sliced
- 2 cups of hand sliced or spiralized Zucchini Noodles
- 1 cup of fresh sliced Mushrooms
- 1 small chopped Red Onion
- 2 cloves of finely chopped Garlic
- 4 fresh, finely chopped Basil Leaves
- 1 tbsp of Basil Pesto Sauce
- 1 tsp Olive Oil

Directions:
1. Sauté the onion in your crockpot or a pan until translucent, then add the garlic and cook until fragrant
2. Then add the mushrooms, chicken, pesto and zucchini noodles stirring to combine
3. If you used a saucepan to sauté, place the mixture in your slow cooker or if you sautéed in your slow cooker, just cover it and cook on the lowest setting, for 8 hours or high for 4 hours
4. Then serve

Nutrition Facts:Per Serving:246 cal, 9g total fat, 2g sat fat, 72mg chol, 172mg sodium, 12g carb, 3g fiber, 31g protein

Fish & Seafood Recipes
Seafood Stew

Servings: 8
Cooking Time: 4 Hours
Ingredients:
- 4 tbsp. olive oil, divided
- 1 onion, diced
- 1 cup carrots, chopped
- 1 cup celery, chopped
- ¼ cup dry white wine
- ¼ tsp dill
- ¼ tsp celery seed
- ½ tsp salt
- ¼ tsp black pepper
- ¼ tsp paprika
- ¼ tsp cayenne pepper
- 3 Yukon gold potatoes, peel & dice
- 2 cups chicken broth, low sodium
- 1 cup water
- 1 tbsp. fresh thyme
- 1 lb. cod, cut in bite-sized pieces
- 20 shrimp, peel, devein & remove tails
- ¼ cup flour
- 2 cups skim milk, divided
- 2 cups skim milk, divided
- 2 tbsp. fresh parsley, chopped

Directions:
1. Heat 2 tablespoons oil in a large skillet over med-high heat.
2. Add onions, carrots, and celery and cook about 5 minutes, or until vegetables start to soften. transfer to the crock pot.
3. stir in the wine and seasonings. Add the lid and cook on high 2 hours.
4. Add the potatoes, broth, water, and thyme, making sure the potatoes are completely covered with liquid. Continue cooking another 60 minutes or until potatoes are tender.
5. Heat remaining oil in a small saucepan over medium heat.
6. slowly whisk in the flour until mixture forms a paste.
7. Whisk in ½ cup milk until mixture is smooth and thickened.
8. Add the fish, shrimp and remaining milk to the crock pot then stir in the roux. Continue cooking another 45-60 minutes or until fish is cooked through. stir in parsley and let rest 30 minutes before serving.

Nutrition Facts:Per Serving: Calories 336, total Carbs 21g, net Carbs 17g, Fiber 4g, Protein 4g, Fat 3g, saturated Fat 2g, sugar 4g, sodium 626mg, Cholesterol 168mg

Exquisite Stuffed Squid

Servings: 2
Cooking Time: 5 Hours
Ingredients:
- 1/2lb of Ripe Tomatoes
- 1 small finely chopped Onion
- 1 clove of crushed Garlic
- 1 medium Red Chili, seeded and finely diced
- 2oz of Dry White Wine
- 1tbsp of Tomato Purée
- 1 fresh or dried Bay Leaves
- ½ a tsp of Fennel Seeds, crushed
- 10.0z of Squid tubes, cut into rings
- 1oz of Green olives, pitted
- The zest of ½ a Lemon
- Olive Oil as Needed
- Flat Leaf Parsley, roughly chopped for garnish

Directions:
1. Puree the tomatoes, then strain them to remove the seeds and skins
2. Sautee the onions until tender
3. Add the tomatoes, tomato purée, bay leaves and fennel seeds
4. Place this mixture with the squid in your crockpot, cook covered for 3 hours on low. Then add the olives, and cook with the lid off to reduce the sauce for 2 hours
5. When the squid is tender, stir in the parsley and lemon zest just and serve with toasted ciabatta or cooked pasta

Nutrition Facts:Per Serving: Cal 284, total fat 8.5g, sat fat 1.5g. sodium 1855mg, carb 11.5g. fiber 4.g, protein 33.3g

Delicious Tuna Mornay

Servings: 2
Cooking Time: 5 Hours
Ingredients:
- ½ a cup of Cream of Mushroom Soup
- ½ a cup of Fresh Cream
- ½ a cup of Tuna in brine (don't drain)
- 1 cup of uncooked Penne Pasta
- ¼ of a cup of frozen Peas
- ¼ of a cup of frozen Corn
- 1 diced Green Onion
- 1/3 of a cup of fresh Water
- ½ a cup of grated Tasty Cheese
- Sea Salt to taste
- Freshly cracked Black Pepper to taste

Directions:
1. Place everything except the cheese into your crockpot and stir to combine well
2. Cook covered on low for 5 hours or for 3 hours on high
3. minutes before serving the Mornay, stir the cheese in

Nutrition Facts:Per Serving: Cal 650, fat 30g, Sodium 790mg, carb 59g, fiber protein , 38g

Tilapia Stew With Green Peppers

Servings:4
Cooking Time: 15 Minutes
Ingredients:
- 1 green bell pepper, medium
- 1 can stewed tomatoes, with Italian seasoning
- 1 lb tilapia
- ½ tbsp seafood seasoning
- 1 cup water
- Cooking spray, nonstick

Directions:
1. Coat your crockpot with cooking spray. Add bell peppers and sauté until lightly brown.
2. Add the tomatoes then simmer until they are tender. Break down the large pieces of the tomatoes.
3. Add tilapia to the pot and stir gently. Lid the crockpot and bring to boil. Reduce heat so that the fish simmers for about three minutes.
4. Remove from heat and let sit for about ten minutes for peak flavors. Serve and enjoy.

Nutrition Facts:Per Serving: Calories 1, Total Fat 2g, Saturated Fat 0.5g, Total Carbs 10g, Net Carbs 7g, Protein 24g, Sugar 6g, Fiber 2g, Sodium 350mg, Potassium 620mg

Creamy Cod & Veggie Soup

Servings: 11
Cooking Time: 5 Hours
Ingredients:
- 2 cups water, divided
- 14 oz. chicken broth, low sodium
- 2 lbs. potatoes, peel & cut in 1/2-inch pieces
- 1 onion, chopped
- 2 stalks celery, chopped
- 1 carrot, chopped
- 1 bay leaf
- 2 (12 oz) cans evaporated milk, fat-free
- 4 tbsp. butter, unsalted
- 1 lb. cod, cut in 1/2-inch pieces
- ½ tsp thyme
- ¼ tsp salt
- ¼ tsp pepper
- 1 tbsp. cornstarch

Directions:
1. Add ½ cups water, broth, potatoes, onion, celery, carrot, and bay leaf to the crock pot. stir to mix.
2. Add the lid and cook on high heat 3 hours, or until potatoes are fork-tender.
3. stir in milk, butter, fish, thyme, salt, and pepper and continue cooking until fish flakes easily with a fork.
4. In a small bowl, whisk together the remaining water and cornstarch until smooth. Add to soup and stir to combine.
5. Cook another 20-30 minutes or until soup has thickened. discard the bay leaf and serve.

Nutrition Facts:Per Serving: Calories 187, total Carbs 22g, net Carbs 20g, Fiber 2g, Protein 13g, Fat 5g, saturated Fat 2g, sugar 9g, sodium 233mg, Cholesterol 31mg

Fisherman's Stew

Servings: 8
Cooking Time: 5 Hours

Ingredients:

- 1 tbsp. olive oil
- ½ lb. mushrooms, sliced
- 2 onions, sliced thin
- 4 cloves garlic, diced fine
- 28 oz. can whole tomatoes, undrained and quartered
- ½ cup dry white wine
- ½ cup clam juice
- 2 tbsp. fresh basil, chopped
- 1 tbsp. oregano
- 1 bay leaf
- ¾ tsp black pepper
- 1 lb. cod, cut in 2-inch pieces
- ½ lb. large shrimp, peel & devein
- 1 lb. little neck clams

Directions:

1. Heat oil in a large skillet over med-high heat.
2. Add mushrooms, onions, and garlic and cook 5 minutes or until vegetables start to soften. transfer to the crock pot.
3. stir in tomatoes, wine, clam juice, and seasonings. Add the lid and cook on high hours, or until mixture comes to a simmer.
4. Add the fish and continue cooking 30 minutes, or until fish is almost done.
5. stir in the shrimp and clams and continue cooking until clams open and shrimp turn pink.
6. discard the bay leaf, stir well and serve.

Nutrition Facts:Per Serving: Calories 121, total Carbs 9g, net Carbs 6g, Fiber 3g, Protein 18g, Fat 1g, saturated Fat 0g, sugar 4g, sodium 449mg, Cholesterol 62mg

Cajun Shrimp Chowder

Servings: 6
Cooking Time: 4 Hours

Ingredients:

- 1 tbsp. butter
- 1 onion, chopped
- 2 cloves garlic, diced fine
- 2 tbsp. flour
- 4 cups cauliflower, separated in florets
- 4 cups chicken broth, low sodium
- 3 thyme sprigs
- ½ tsp paprika
- 2 green onions, sliced
- 3 cups corn
- ¾ cups heavy cream
- 6 slices bacon, chopped
- 1 lb. shrimp, tails removed
- 2 tsp Cajun seasoning

Directions:

1. Melt butter in a large skillet over medium heat.
2. Add onion and cook until soft, about 5 minutes.
3. stir in garlic and flour and cook about seconds, stirring constantly.
4. Add cauliflower, broth, thyme, paprika, and ¾ of green onions to the crock pot. stir in the garlic mixture until combined.
5. Add lid and cook on low heat 4 hours, or until cauliflower is fork-tender.
6. stir in the corn and cream until combined. Cook another 30- minutes.
7. Heat a large skillet over med-high heat. Add bacon and cook until crisp. transfer to a paper towel-lined plate.
8. sprinkle shrimp with Cajun seasoning and add to the skillet and cook until pink, about 2 minutes per side. transfer to plate with the bacon.
9. When the chowder is done, stir in the shrimp. Ladle chowder into bowls and top with crumbled bacon and remaining green onions.

Nutrition Facts:Per Serving: Calories 338, total Carbs 24g, net Carbs 20g, Fiber 4g, Protein 25g, Fat 18g, saturated Fat 4g, sugar , sodium 1010mg, Cholesterol 141mg

Sophia Homemade Crockpot Seafood Stock

Servings:10
Cooking Time: 4 Hours 20 Minutes
Ingredients:
- 4 carrots, coarsely chopped
- 1 bunch celery, coarsely chopped
- 2 green bell peppers, coarsely chopped
- ½ lb fish parts, bones and tail + 2 fish heads
- 2 cups clam juice
- 1 tbsp olive oil
- 2 onions, coarsely chopped
- 1 bunch cilantro, fresh
- ½ bunch oregano, fresh
- 2 bay leaves
- 1 ½ bottles water
- 1 tbsp whole black peppercorns

Directions:
1. Heat olive oil in your crockpot. Stir cook onions for five minutes then add carrots, celery, and peppers.
2. Sauté for five more minutes, then add the spices. Sauté for two additional minutes.
3. Add water, fish parts and heads, clam juice, and peppercorns to the crockpot.
4. Bring mixture to boil then cook on low for four hours. Turn off the heat and let rest for thirty minutes.
5. Strain the stock using a fine mesh strainer so that all fish bones are removed.
6. Serve and enjoy.

Nutrition Facts:Per Serving: Calories 55, Total Fat 1., Saturated Fat 0g, Total Carbs 9.2g, Net Carbs 6.4g, Protein 1.6g, Sugar 4g, Fiber 2.8g, Sodium 182mg, Potassium 446mg

Magical Coconut Cilantro Currie Shrimp

Servings: 2
Cooking Time: 2 Hours
Ingredients:
- ½lb of Raw Shrimp, peeled and deveined
- 15oz of Coconut Milk
- 7.5oz of Fresh Water
- 1 tbsp of Red Curry Paste
- 1 tsp of Lemon-Garlic Seasoning
- ¼ of a cup of chopped Cilantro

Directions:
1. Place everything except the shrimp in your crockpot and cook covered on high for 2 hours
2. Add the shrimp and cook another 30 minutes
3. Garnish with the Cilantro and serve

Nutrition Facts:Per Serving: Cal 529, total fat53g, Chol 16mg, Sodium7g, Carb14g, Fiber4.8g Protein 6.7g

Rich Crab, Spinach And Egg Casserole

Servings:2
Cooking Time: 10 Minutes
Ingredients:
- 2 Fresh Eggs
- ½ a cup of full Cream
- A 6oz can of Crabmeat, drained
- 3oz of frozen and chopped Spinach, thawed and then squeezed dry
- ¼ of a cup of dry Breadcrumbs
- 1oz of your favorite tasty, shredded, Italian Cheese
- Sea Salt to taste
- Freshly ground Black Pepper to taste
- ¼ of a tsp of freshly ground Nutmeg
- 1 Celery Stalk including Leaves, chopped
- ¼ of a cup of diced Onion
- ¼ of a cup of diced Red Capsicum
- 1 medium sized fresh diced Mushroom
- 1 tbsp of Olive Oil

Directions:
1. Whisk the eggs and cream together
2. Stir in the crab, spinach, bread crumbs, cheese and nutmeg
3. Season it with salt and pepper and set it aside
4. Sauté the onion, capsicum and mushrooms until tender
5. Combine everything and place it in your crockpot
6. Cook covered on high for 3 to 4 hours or low 5 to hours

Nutrition Facts:Per Serving: Cal 163, fat 9g, sat fat 5g, carb 8g, chol 141mg, sodium 265mg, fiber 1g, protein 10g

Manhattan Clam Chowder

Servings: 6
Cooking Time: 4 Hours
Ingredients:
- 2 tbsp. olive oil
- 1 onion, chopped
- 2 stalks celery, chopped
- 2 carrots, peel & chop
- 2 potatoes, peel & dice
- 2 (14 ½ oz) cans tomatoes, diced, undrained
- 2 (10 oz) cans baby clams, undrained
- 2 (8 oz) bottles clam juice
- 2 slices bacon, cooked crisp & crumbled
- 1 tsp thyme

Directions:
1. Heat oil in a large skillet over med-high heat.
2. Add onion, celery, and carrots and cook 5-7 minutes or until onions soften. transfer to crock pot.
3. Add remaining ingredients and stir to mix well.
4. Add lid and cook on low heat 3-hours or until potatoes are tender. serve immediately.

Nutrition Facts:Per Serving: Calories 146, total Carbs 22g, net Carbs 17g, Fiber , Protein 9g, Fat 5g, saturated Fat 1g, sugar 7g, sodium 882mg, Cholesterol 4mg

Delicate Shrimp With Tomatoes And Feta

Servings:2
Cooking Time: 4.5 Hours
Ingredients:
- ½lb of medium sized Shrimp, shelled and deveined
- 1 small chopped Onion
- ½ a cup of Crushed Tomatoes
- ½ a cup of Dry White Wine (a nice drinking wine)
- 1/8 of a tsp of dried Oregano
- Sea Salt to taste
- A pinch of Crushed Red Pepper
- 1 cup of crumbled Feta Cheese
- 2 tbsp of fresh Flat-Leaf Parsley, chopped
- 1 tbsp of Extra-Virgin Olive Oil

Directions:
1. Place all the ingredients except the shrimp and feta cheese into your crockpot and cook covered for 2 hours or low for 4 hours
2. Stir the shrimps into the sauce, then add the feta cheese and serve on couscous sprinkled with chopped parsley

Nutrition Facts:Per Serving: Cal 3g, total fat 10g, sat fat 4.7g, chol 428mg, sodium 787mg, carb 5.1g, fiber 1.2g, protein 47.8g

Succulent Salmon With Caramelized Onions

Servings:4
Cooking Time: 20 Minutes
Ingredients:
- 1 lb salmon
- ½ sweet onion
- ¼ tbsp ginger, ground
- ¼ tbsp dried dill
- ½ lemon, sliced
- 1 tbsp olive oil
- ¼ salt
- 1/8 tbsp pepper

Directions:
1. Cut salmon into desired pieces, and that will fit into the crockpot.
2. Place the onions at the bottom of the crockpot. Foil each salmon piece in a different paper foil enough to be folded like a packet.
3. Sprinkle spices over the salmon pieces and top with lemon. Fold the paper foil into packets and stack them on the onions.
4. Set the timer for six hours on low. When the time elapses, remove the salmon from packets and top with onions.
5. Serve and enjoy.

Nutrition Facts:Per Serving: Calories 215, Total Fat 11g, Saturated Fat 2g, Total Carbs 7g, Net Carbs 5g, Protein 24g, Sugar 3g, Fiber 2g, Sodium 200mg, Potassium 520mg

Royal Lobster Tails

Servings:2
Cooking Time: 2 Hours
Ingredients:
- ½lb of fresh Lobster tails
- ½ a cup of Water
- ½ a stick of Unsalted Butter
- ½ a tsp of Garlic Salt

Directions:
1. Place everything into your crockpot and cook covered for 2 hours on high and serve with your favorite dipping sauce or garlic butter

Nutrition Facts:Per Serving: Cal 510, total fat 45.8g, sat fat g, chol 191mg, sodium 706mg, carb1.1g, fiber 0.1g protein 24.7g

Mediterranean Calamari Stew

Servings: 2
Cooking Time: 4 Hours
Ingredients:
- 1/2lb of Calamari Tubes
- 1 small diced Onions
- 1 clove of minced Garlic
- 1 Chili Pepper
- 1 tbsp of Capers
- 6 large Black Olives
- 2 tbsp of Tomato Paste
- ½ a cup of Diced Tomatoes
- 3 sprigs of fresh Thyme
- 1 Bay Leaf
- Sea Salt to taste
- Freshly cracked Black Pepper to taste
- 1 tbsp of Olive Oil

Directions:
1. Cut the calamari tubes to about 8th inch thick
2. Place the onions, thyme sprigs, bay leaves, chili, tomato paste, tomatoes, and garlic in your crockpot
3. Cook covered on high for 2.5 hours or low for 4 hours
4. Dice the capers, finely and slice the olives into rings and add them with the calamari to your crockpot, then add these to your slow cooker with the calamari rings
5. Cook covered on high another hour, then remove the bay leaves and thyme
6. Taste and then serve

Nutrition Facts:Per Serving: Cal 430, total fat 21.4g, sat fat 3.3g, chol 528mg, sodium 809mg, fiber 4.4g, protein 38.8g

Shrimp & Sausage Pot

Servings: 6
Cooking Time: 4 Hours
Ingredients:
- 8 cups water
- ½ tbsp. seafood seasoning
- 1/8 tsp cayenne pepper
- 4 cloves garlic, chopped
- 1/2 pound turkey kielbasa sausage, cut into1-1/2-inch pieces
- 3 red potatoes, cut in quarters
- 1 onion, cut into chunks
- 2 ears corn, cut into 3-inch pieces
- 12 ounces jumbo shrimp, unpeeled

Directions:
1. stir together water, seasonings, and garlic in the crock pot.
2. Add kielbasa, potatoes, onions, and corn.
3. Add lid and cook on high heat 4 hours or until potatoes are fork-tender.
4. Add shrimp and continue cooking another 30 minutes, or until shrimp turn pink.
5. Ladle into bowls and serve immediately.

Nutrition Facts:Per Serving: Calories 21 total Carbs 22g, net Carbs 20g, Fiber 2g, Protein 15g, Fat 8g, saturated Fat 2g, sugar 3g, sodium 967mg, Cholesterol 98mg

Heavenly Seafood Chowder

Servings: 2
Cooking Time: 5 Hours
Ingredients:
- 2 thick slices of Smoked Bacon
- 1 small diced Onion
- 1 clove of diced Garlic
- 2 cups of Chicken or Seafood Stock
- ½ a cup of Corn Kernels
- 1 stalk of sliced Celery Leaves included
- 1 large diced Potato
- 1 small diced Carrot
- ½ a cup of Raw Scallops
- ½ a cup of medium Prawns, Peeled
- ½ a cup of small Mussels, shelled
- ½ a cup of Halibut or Cod, sliced into ½ in cubes
- 1 tbsp of Tomato Paste

Directions:
1. Place everything except the seafood in your crockpot and cook covered for 3 hours
2. Then add the seafood and cook another hour
3. Serve garnished with fresh herbs

Nutrition Facts:Per Serving: Cal 235, fat 6g, carb 27.9g, sodium 72g, chol 56mg, protein 18.4g

Stunning Seafood Casserole

Servings: 2
Cooking Time: 5.5 Hours
Ingredients:
- ½ a cup of diced tomatoes
- 1 small diced Onion
- 1 chopped stalk of Celery
- ¼lb of cubed Haddock Fillets
- 1/4lb raw Shrimp, peeled and deveined
- 6oz can of Chopped Clams, drained
- 6oz Crabmeat, drained
- 4oz Clam Juice
- ¼ of a cup of Dry White Wine
- 2oz Tomato Paste
- 2 cloves of crushed Garlic
- 1 tsp of Italian Seasoning
- 1 Bay Leaf
- 1 tbsp of fresh minced Parsley

Directions:
1. Place everything except the haddock, clams, shrimp and crabmeat in your crockpot and cook covered on low for 5 hours
2. Add the haddock, clams, shrimp and crabmeat and cook, covered another 30 minutes
3. Take out the bay leaf and add the parsley then serve

Nutrition Facts:Per Serving: Cal 236, Fat 1g, Chol 36mg, Sodium 1789mg, Carb31g, fiber , Protein 22g

Creole Shrimp & Peppers

Servings: 4
Cooking Time: 4 Hours
Ingredients:
- 1 cup onion, diced
- 1 cup green bell pepper, chopped
- 1 cup celery, chopped
- 2 tbsp. fresh parsley, chopped
- 15 oz. tomato sauce, low sodium
- ½ cup water
- ½ tsp Creole seasoning
- ¾ lb. medium shrimp, peel, devein & remove tails

Directions:
1. Add vegetables to the crock pot. Pour in tomato sauce, water, and seasonings and stir to mix.
2. Add lid and cook on high heat 3-4 hours, or until vegetables are tender.
3. stir in shrimp and cook until they turn pink. serve immediately.

Nutrition Facts:Per Serving: Calories 120, total Carbs 1, net Carbs 12g, Fiber 2g, Protein 13g, Fat 1g, saturated Fat 0g, sugar 8g, sodium 561mg, Cholesterol 107mg

Seafood Gumbo Stock

Servings:8
Cooking Time: 7 Hours 30 Minutes
Ingredients:
- 1 lb shrimp shells
- 4 carrots, sliced
- ½ bunch celery, sliced
- 2 bay leaves
- 2 sprigs parsley, fresh
- 5 cups water
- 4 onions
- 3 garlic cloves, sliced
- 5 garlic cloves, whole
- 1 tbsp black pepper, ground
- 1 tbsp dried basil
- 2 tbsp dried thyme

Directions:
1. Preheat oven to 3750F.
2. Bake the shrimps until the edges start to brown.
3. Add all the ingredients to the crockpot and bring to boil.
4. Reduce heat, lid, and set time for six hours. Replace water two to three times as needed.
5. Remove stock from the crockpot and strain. Press liquid from all shells and vegetables then discard them.
6. Return stock to the crockpot and heat until it is reduced to eight cups.
7. Serve and enjoy.

Nutrition Facts:Per Serving: Calories 112, Total Fat 1.3g, Saturated Fat 0g, Total Carbs 12.1g, Net Carbs 9g, Protein 13.2g, Sugar 5g, Fiber 3.3g, Sodium 162mg, Potassium 464mg

Simple Poached Salmon

Servings:4
Cooking Time: 1 Hour 20 Minutes
Ingredients:
- 1 onion, sliced1 celery rib, sliced
- 1 carrot, sliced
- 3 thyme sprigs, fresh
- 1 rosemary sprig, fresh
- 24 oz salmon fillet
- 2 cups water
- 1 cup white wine
- 2 tbsp lemon juice
- 1 bay leaf
- ½ tbsp salt
- ¼ tbsp pepper
- Lemon wedges

Directions:
1. Add all the ingredients in your crockpot except salmon and lemon wedges.
2. Place the lid and set time for forty-five minutes.
3. When time elapses, add the salmon fillets and add water until the salmon is covered.
4. Cook until the salmon easily flakes or for forty-five minutes.
5. Remove fish from cooking liquids and serve with lemon wedges. Enjoy

Nutrition Facts:Per Serving: Calories 272, Total Fat 1, Saturated Fat 3g, Total Carbs 1g, Net Carbs 0g, Protein 29g, Sugar 0g, Fiber 0g, Sodium 115mg, Potassium 320mg

Supreme Salmon

Servings:2
Cooking Time: 6 Hours
Ingredients:
- 1/2lb of Salmon Fillets
- 2 cloves of finely sliced Garlic
- 1 small finely sliced Onion
- 1 finely sliced Zucchini
- 1 finely sliced Red Capsicum
- 1 large ripe finely diced Tomato
- ½ a tsp of Garlic Powder
- ½ a tsp of Onion Powder
- ½ a tsp of Italian Seasoning
- ¼ of a tsp of freshly cracked Black Pepper
- 4 rings of sliced Lemon
- Sea Salt to taste
- 1 tbsp of Olive Oil

Directions:
1. Oil a small casserole dish with a tight fitting lid that fits inside your crockpot
2. Place the salmon fillets inside the casserole and season it with one half of the onion powder, garlic powder, Italian seasoning, pepper and salt
3. Spread the garlic, onion, zucchini, capsicum and tomato around the salmon and add the rest of the seasoning
4. Place 2 lemon rings on each piece of salmon
5. Place the lid on your casserole dish and then place it inside your crockpot with a cup of water
6. Cook covered for hours on the low setting

Nutrition Facts:Per Serving: Cal 225, total fat 11.8g, sat fat 1., chol 52mg, sodium 59mg, 8 carb.1g, fiber 1.6g, protein 23.5g

Tender Galician Octopus

Servings: 2
Cooking Time: 5 Hours
Ingredients:
- 1 medium Octopus
- Sea Salt
- Fresh water
- Boiled Potatoes

Directions:
1. Remove the octopus head, discard it or use it to make stock
2. Have a large stock pot filled with boiling water
3. With the water at a rolling boil, dip the whole octopus in the water for about 15 seconds
4. This will "shock" the legs, causing them to curl up so the skin will then remain on while the octopus is cooking. Continue dipping it until the legs have curled up completely
5. Place the octopus in your crockpot
6. Cover it with fresh water and add 1 tbsp of sea salt
7. Cook it covered on the high setting for 5 hours or low for8 hours
8. To check if it is done, pierce with a skewer or fork the thick part of the leg
9. Remove from the crockpot and slice the legs thinly and serve with potato slices

Nutrition Facts:Per Serving: Cal 139, total fat 1.8g, sat fat 0.4g, chol 82mg, sodium 391mg, carb 3.7g, protein 25.4g

Lovely Poached Whole Snapper With Fennel And Pernod

Servings: 2
Cooking Time: 8 Hours

Ingredients:

- 2 plate sized whole Snapper, with the gills, gut and scales removed
- 1 head of Fennel
- 2 sprigs of Thyme
- 2 sprigs of Oregano
- 1 lemon, thinly sliced
- 2 tbsp of Extra-Virgin Olive Oil
- Sea Salt to taste
- Freshly cracked Black Pepper as needed
- 1/2 a cup of fresh Water
- The juice of 1 fresh Lemon
- 1 tbsp of Pernod or Ouzo
- The leaves from the fresh Fennel
- 3 tbsp of Unsalted Butter
- Sea Salt to taste
- Freshly cracked Black Pepper

Directions:

1. Season the fish inside, using salt and pepper
2. Place half the tender green fennel heads and a sprig of thyme and oregano inside each fish and slice the fennel bulb
3. Place ½ a cup of water into the crockpot
4. Make 3 slices diagonally down to the bone on each side of each fish and place a slice of lemon in each cut
5. Brush each fish with olive oil and season it with sea salt and pepper
6. Place the fish on a stand in your crockpot with the sliced fennel bulb
7. Cook covered on high for 3 hours or low for 5 hours or until the fish flesh becomes opaque
8. Remove the fish with the stand and let it rest while you make the sauce
9. Place the lemon juice and Pernod in a saucepan with the liquid from the crockpot and simmer this to reduce it by about one third then turn off the heat
10. Chop the remaining fennel leaves finely
11. The sauce should have cooled slightly so whisk in the six tbsp of butter and then add the fennel leaves
12. Taste and adjust the seasoning if necessary
13. Serve the fish with the Pernod sauce and fennel

Nutrition Facts:Per Serving: Cal 649, total fat 51.1g, sat fat 1.1g, chol 60mg, sodium 137mg, carb 11.3g, fiber 4.9g, protein 35.1g

Halibut Chowder

Servings: 8
Cooking Time: 4 Hours
Ingredients:
- 2 stalks celery, chopped
- 2 carrots, chopped
- 1 onion, chopped
- 2 (14 ½ oz) cans tomatoes, diced, undrained
- 2 (14 ½ oz) cans chicken broth, low sodium
- 1 tsp thyme
- ¼ tsp black pepper
- 1 lb. halibut, cut in 1-inch pieces

Directions:
1. Place the celery, carrots, and onion in the crock pot.
2. Add tomatoes, broth, thyme and pepper and stir to mix.
3. Add the lid and cook on high heat 2-hours or until carrots are tender.
4. Add the halibut and cook another 60 minutes, or until fish flakes easily. serve immediately.

Nutrition Facts:Per Serving: Calories 12 total Carbs 10g, net Carbs 8g, Fiber 2g, Protein 12g, Fat 5g, saturated Fat 1g, sugar 5g, sodium 143mg, Cholesterol 31mg

Simple Steamed Crab Legs

Servings:4
Cooking Time: 15 Minutes
Ingredients:
- 2 lb king crab legs, frozen
- 1 lemon juice
- ⅓ Cup melted butter
- 1 ½ cups water

Directions:
1. Place the trivet in the crockpot then add water. Place the crab legs on the trivet; thaw them first if they do not fit the crockpot.
2. Set the timer for ten minutes on high pressure. When time is done, remove the crab legs from the crockpot.
3. Sprinkle lemon juice on top and serve with melted butter. Enjoy.

Nutrition Facts:Per Serving: Calories 199, Total Fat 16g, Saturated Fat 10g, Total Carbs 1.2g, Net Carbs 0g, Protein 12.7g, Sugar 0g, Fiber 0g, Sodium 32g, Potassium 244mg

Spicy Halibut Stew

Servings: 6
Cooking Time: 8 Hours
Ingredients:
- 1 red bell pepper, chopped
- 1 onion, chopped
- 2 carrots, sliced thin
- 1 large potato, peel & cut in 1-inch pieces
- 1 ½ cups chicken broth, low sodium
- Juice from 1 lime
- 2 cloves garlic, diced
- ½ teaspoon black pepper
- ½ tsp salt
- 1 tsp chili powder
- ¼ cup + 2 tbsp. cilantro, chopped
- ½ tsp cumin
- ½ tsp red pepper flakes
- 1 lb. halibut, cut in bite-size pieces

Directions:
1. Combine all ingredients, except halibut and the 2 tablespoons cilantro in the crock pot.
2. Add lid and cook on low heat 7 hours.
3. Add halibut and cook another -60 minutes or until fish flakes easily.
4. Ladle into bowls, garnish with more cilantro and serve.

Nutrition Facts:Per Serving: Calories 148, total Carbs 12g, net Carbs 10g, Fiber 2g, Protein 18g, Fat 2g, saturated Fat 1g, sugar 4g, sodium 296mg, Cholesterol 46mg

10-minute Crockpot Salmon

Servings:4
Cooking Time: 5minutes
Ingredients:
- 3 lemon
- 4 salmon fillets
- 1 bunch fresh dill weed
- ¾ cup water
- 1 tbsp butter, unsalted
- ¼ tbsp salt
- ¼ tbsp ground black pepper

Directions:
1. Add a quarter cup lemon juice with three quarter cup water to the crockpot.
2. Place a steamer basket in place and place the salmon fillets on top.
3. Sprinkle dill weed and place a lemon slice on each salmon fillet.
4. Lid the crockpot and set time for five minutes. Remove the salmon from the crockpot and serve with butter, more dill, and lemon, salt, and pepper to taste. Enjoy.

Nutrition Facts:Per Serving: Calories 441, Total Fat 30g, Saturated Fat 9g, Total Carbs 12g, Net Carbs 8g, Protein 36g, Sugar 3g, Fiber 4g, Sodium 402mg, Potassium 426mg

Mediterranean Chili Crab

Servings: 2
Cooking Time: 2 Hours
Ingredients:
- 1/4lb of fresh or frozen Crab Meat
- 2 whole fresh Crabs
- 1 or 2 Chili peppers, depending on how hot you like it, chopped
- 1/4 inch piece of grated fresh Ginger
- 2 cloves of chopped Garlic
- 2 chopped Spring Onions (Green Onions)
- 1 tsp of ground Dried Coriander
- 2 tsp of fresh Lime Zest
- Sea Salt to taste
- 1 teaspoon shrimp paste
- 1 cup of Cashew Milk or Coconut Cream
- 1 tbsp of Fish Sauce
- 1 or 2 fresh Lime leaves
- Fresh cracked Black Pepper to taste
- 2 tbsp of Cilantro, chopped as a garnish

Directions:
1. Blend together the ginger, garlic, chili, shallots, ground coriander, lime zest, and shrimp paste to a smooth paste
2. Place the paste with the cashew milk in your crockpot and cook covered on high for about an hour
3. Add the whole crabs, crab meat, fish sauce and lime leaves to the mixture in your crockpot and cook a further hour
4. Check the seasoning and add salt and pepper if necessary
5. Serve over quinoa with the chopped cilantro as a garnish

Nutrition Facts:Per Serving: Cal 353, Fat 21, Sat fat 17g, unsat 1g, Cho mg, Carb 25g, Fiber4g, Protein 22g

Greek Cod With Olives And Tomatoes

Servings:2
Cooking Time: 4 Hours
Ingredients:
- ½lb of fresh Cod Fillets
- ½ a cup of diced Tomatoes
- 2 tbsp of Kalamata Olives
- ¼ of a cup of Dry White Wine
- 1 tbsp of Olive Oil
- 1 clove of minced Garlic
- ¼ of a tsp of dried Oregano
- ¼ a tsp of Fennel Seeds, lightly crushed
- 1/8 of a tsp of crushed Red Pepper

Directions:
1. Sauté the garlic, fennel seed, red pepper and oregano until fragrant in the oil
2. Add the wine, olives and tomatoes and cook in your crockpot, covered, for 1 hour on high or 3 hours on low
3. Add the cod fillets and cook about another hour or until the fish is tender and flakes easily with a fork
4. Serve the cod on quinoa and pour the sauce from your crockpot over the top

Nutrition Facts:Per Serving: Cal 8, total fat 29.8g, sat fat 5.4g, chol 58mg, sodium 1214mg, carb 39.6g, fiber 4.4g, protein 26.7g

Beef, Pork & Lamb Recipes

Lamb And Lentil Shepherd's Pie

Servings: 2
Cooking Time: 8 Hours
Ingredients:
- ¼lb of ground Lamb, Beef or Pork
- 1 small diced Onion
- ¼ of a cup of frozen Mixed Vegetables
- ½ a cup of Stock or Broth
- ½ a cup of diced Tomatoes
- ¼ of a cup of low fat, reduced Sodium Tomato Soup
- ¼ of a cup of rinsed and drained Brown Lentils
- 1/8 of a tsp of Red Pepper Flakes
- 1 cup of Mashed Potatoes

Directions:
1. Combine everything except the mashed potato in your crockpot and mix well
2. Spread the mashed potato over the top of the mixture
3. Cook, covered, for 8 hours and serve with your favorite chopped herbs

Nutrition Facts:Per Serving: Cal 960, Fat 12.7g, chol 325mg, sodium 1119mg, Carb .3g, fiber 6g, protein 110.5g

Fabulous Chili Con Carne

Servings:2
Cooking Time: 8 Hours
Ingredients:
- 1/2lb of Ground Lean Beef
- 1 small finely chopped Onion
- ½ of a cup of Whole Kernel Corn
- 1 clove of minced Garlic
- ½ a cup of Tomato Sauce
- 2 tbsp of Tomato Paste
- 1 cup of cans of Diced Tomatoes
- ½ a cup of Chili Beans
- ½ a cup of Beef Stock
- 1 tsp of ground Cumin
- 1 tsp of Paprika
- 1 tsp of Chili Powder or more if you like it hotter
- 1 tsp of Oregano
- Sea Salt to taste
- Ground Black Pepper to taste
- 1 tbsp of Coconut Oil

Directions:
1. Place everything in your crockpot and mix it evenly, then cook, covered, on low for 8 hours

Nutrition Facts:Per Serving: Cal 4, total fat 17.5g, sat fat 8.4g, chol 111mg, sodium 1528mg, carb 25.5g, fiber 6.7g, protein 42.6g

Sassy Pot Roast

Servings:8
Cooking Time: 8 Hours
Ingredients:

- 2 pounds beef chuck roast
- 1 tbsp Worcestershire sauce
- 8 ounces tomato sauce
- 2tbsp brown sugar
- ¼ cup ketchup
- ½ tbsp pepper
- ½ tbsp salt
- 1 chopped onion, large
- ¼ cup lemon juice
- ¼ cup cider vinegar
- 2 tbsp olive oil
- ¼ cup water
- ½ tbsp mustard, ground
- ½ tbsp paprika

Directions:
1. Splash the beef with pepper and salt.
2. Add in a skillet, large, then brown the beef on all sides. Drain.
3. Transfer the beef to a crockpot then add the onions.
4. Meanwhile, combine all the remaining ingredients in a mixing bowl and pour over the beef.
5. Cover the crockpot and cook for about 8-10 hours on low. Cook until tender then skim fat.
6. Thicken cooking liquid if desired.
7. Serve.

Nutrition Facts:Per Serving: Calories: 243, total fat: 12g, saturated fat: 9g, total carbs: 10g, net carbs: 9g, protein: 23g, sugars: 7g, fiber: 1g, sodium: 443mg, potassium: 2mg

Beef And Tomato Lasagna

Servings: 2
Cooking Time: 6 Hours
Ingredients:

- ¼lb of Lean Ground Beef
- 1 small chopped Onion
- 1 clove of chopped Garlic
- ½ a cup of Tomato Salsa
- ½ a cup of Tomato Paste
- ½ a cup of Italian Stewed Tomatoes
- ¼ of a pack of Whole Wheat Lasagna Noodles
- 6oz of Ricotta Cheese
- 2oz of grated Parmesan Cheese
- 4oz of Mozzarella Cheese
- ½ a tsp of Dried Oregano
- ½ a tbsp of Italian Seasoning
- Sea Salt to taste
- Freshly ground Black Pepper to taste

Directions:
1. Combine the beef, Italian seasoning, oregano, garlic, onions, tomato salsa, paste, stewed tomato and ¼ of a tsp of salt and bring to a simmer in a saucepan
2. Combine the cheeses in a bowl
3. Assemble the lasagna by placing a small amount of meat sauce on the bottom of your crockpot. Then add a layer of lasagna Noodles (uncooked), break them to get a good fit
4. Then add a layer of the cheese, followed by a layer of spinach
5. Add another layer of meat and then noodles, cheese, spinach, meat, followed by another layer of noodles and a final layer of cheese
6. Cook, covered, for hours on low

Nutrition Facts:Per Serving: Cal 516, carb 21.3g, total fat 26.2g, sat fat 15., Cho 114mg, sodium 887mg fiber 2.5g, Protien 47g

Homemade Pork & Beans

Servings: 12
Cooking Time: 6 Hours
Ingredients:
- 3 lbs. pork loin chops
- 2 (15 oz) cans pinto beans, undrained
- ¼ cup molasses
- ½ cup ketchup, sugar-free
- 1 tsp garlic powder
- 1 tbsp. onion powder
- 1 tbsp. apple cider vinegar

Directions:
1. Place the pork in the crock pot.
2. Pour the beans, with their liquid, over the pork.
3. Add remaining ingredients and stir to mix.
4. Add the lid and cook on low heat 6 hours, or until pork begins to fall apart.
5. Remove the chops from the crock pot and cut or shred them. Return the meat to the beans, stir to combine and serve.

Nutrition Facts:Per Serving: Calories 243, total Carbs 19g, net Carbs 1, Fiber 3g, Protein 31g, Fat 5g, saturated Fat 1g, sugar 6g, sodium 557mg, Cholesterol 58mg

Bbq Pork Chops & Peppers

Servings: 4
Cooking Time: 6 Hours
Ingredients:
- nonstick cooking spray
- 4 pork chops, boneless, 1-inch thick
- 1 ½ tsp garlic powder, divided
- ¼ tsp black pepper
- 1 red bell pepper, cut in 1/2-inch slices
- 1 onion, sliced thin
- 1 cup mushrooms, quartered
- ½ cup ketchup, sugar-free
- ¼ cup cider vinegar
- 1 tbsp. molasses
- 1 tsp paprika
- 1 tsp cayenne pepper
- 1 tsp onion powder

Directions:
1. spray a large skillet with cooking spray and heat over med-high heat.
2. sprinkle the pork with ½ teaspoon garlic and pepper. Add to the skillet and cook until brown on both sides.
3. Place the bell pepper, onion, and mushrooms in the crock pot. Place the pork chops on the vegetables.
4. In a small bowl, whisk together the remaining ingredients until smooth. Pour over the pork chops.
5. Add the lid and cook on low heat 4-6 hours, or until pork is tender. serve.

Nutrition Facts:Per Serving: Calories 204, total Carbs 18g, net Carbs 1, Fiber 2g, Protein 25g, Fat 4g, saturated Fat 1g, sugar 13g, sodium 414mg, Cholesterol 63mg

Burgundy Braised Lamb Shanks

Servings: 4
Cooking Time: 8 Hours
Ingredients:
- 4 lamb shanks
- 1 tsp salt
- 1 tsp pepper
- 2 tbsp. parsley
- 2 tsp garlic, diced fine
- ½ tsp oregano
- ½ tsp lemon zest, grated
- 1 tsp olive oil
- ½ cup onion, chopped
- 1 carrot, chopped
- 1 cup Burgundy wine
- 1 tsp beef bouillon granules

Directions:
1. sprinkle the lamb with salt and pepper and place in crock pot. sprinkle parsley, garlic, oregano, and zest over the top.
2. Heat oil in a small saucepan over medium heat. Add onion and carrot and cook 3-4 minutes or until onion starts to soften.
3. stir in wine and bouillon and bring to a boil, stirring occasionally. Pour over lamb.
4. Add the lid and cook on low heat 8 hours or until lamb is tender.
5. transfer lamb to serving plate and keep warm. Pour cooking liquid into a saucepan and skim off fat. Bring to a boil and cook until reduced by half. serve lamb topped with sauce.

Nutrition Facts:Per Serving: Calories 771, total Carbs , net Carbs 5g, Fiber 1g, Protein 69g, Fat 23g, saturated Fat 7g, sugar 1g, sodium 775mg, Cholesterol 369mg

Perfection In A Pot Roast

Servings: 2
Cooking Time: 8 Hours
Ingredients:
- 1lb Beef Rump Roast
- 1 packet of Onion Soup Mix
- Black Pepper to taste
- 2 cups of Fresh Water

Directions:
1. Place everything in your crockpot and cook, covered, on low for 8 hours

Nutrition Facts:Per Serving: Cal,341, Fat 8g, Sodium 577mg, Carb., Fiber 8g, Protein 32g

Classic Roadhouse Chili

Servings: 8
Cooking Time: 8 Hours
Ingredients:
- 1 ½ lbs. lean ground beef
- 1 sweet onion, chopped
- 2 (15 oz) cans kidney beans, drain & rinse
- 15 oz. can black beans, drain & rinse
- 14 ½ oz. tomatoes, diced
- 6 oz. tomato paste
- 2 ½ tbsp. chili powder
- ½ tsp pepper
- 1 tsp salt
- ½ tsp crushed red pepper flakes
- 1 cup tomato
- 2 ½ cups water

Directions:
1. In a large skillet over med-high heat cook beef, breaking up with a spatula, until no longer pink. drain off fat and transfer to the crock pot.
2. Add remaining ingredients and stir to mix well.
3. Add the lid and cook on low heat 6-8 hours. stir well before serving.

Nutrition Facts:Per Serving: Calories 253, total Carbs 32g, net Carbs 21g, Fiber 11g, Protein 20g, Fat 6g, saturated Fat 2g, sugar 7g, sodium 671mg, Cholesterol mg

Kielbasa (polish Sausage) With Cabbage And Potatoes

Servings:2
Cooking Time: 8 Hours
Ingredients:
- ½lb Kielbasa, sliced into rings
- 2 cups of Green Cabbage, sliced into thin strips
- 1 small diced Potato
- 1 small finely diced Onion
- ¼ of a tsp of Caraway Seeds
- ¼ of a tsp of Sea Salt
- 6oz of Chicken Stock

Directions:
1. Place everything in your crockpot and stir to mix, then cook, covered, on low for hours, then serve

Nutrition Facts:Per Serving: Cal 378, Total fat, 15g, sat fat 4g, Sodium 7mg, Carb 22g Fier 5g, Protein 37g

Beef & Cabbage Stew

Servings: 6
Cooking Time: 6 Hours
Ingredients:
- 1 lb. lean ground beef
- 1 onion, chopped
- 15 oz. tomatoes, stewed
- 15 oz. tomato sauce, no added salt
- 2 cloves garlic, diced fine
- 1 tbsp. Worcestershire sauce
- 1 cup beef broth, low sodium
- 1 tsp black pepper
- ½ tsp crushed red pepper flakes
- ½ head cabbage, chopped

Directions:
1. In a large skillet over medium heat, cook beef and onions until meat is no longer pink.
2. Add the tomatoes, tomato sauce, garlic, Worcestershire, broth, and seasonings to the crock pot. stir to combine.
3. Add the beef and cabbage and mix together.
4. Add the lid and cook on low heat 5-6 hours. stir before serving.

Nutrition Facts:Per Serving: Calories 242, total Carbs 14g, net Carbs 11g, Fiber 3g, Protein 17g, Fat 13g, saturated Fat 0g, sugar 6g, sodium 143mg, Cholesterol 0mg

Tuscan-style Pork Chops

Servings: 6
Cooking Time: 8 Hours
Ingredients:
- 2 tsp Italian seasoning
- 4 cloves garlic, diced fine
- ½ tsp salt
- ¼ tsp pepper
- 1 onion, chopped
- 6 bone-in pork chops,1/2-inch thick
- 2 (14 ½ oz) cans tomatoes, diced & undrained
- 2 tbsp. balsamic vinegar
- 2 zucchini, cut in 1-inch pieces
- 2 tbsp. cornstarch
- 2 tbsp. water
- 4 oz. orzo, cooked

Directions:
1. In a small bowl, combine Italian seasoning, garlic, salt, and pepper. stir to mix.
2. Place the onion in the crock pot.
3. Add half the pork chops and sprinkle with half the seasoning mixture. Repeat.
4. Pour in the tomatoes, vinegar and zucchini.
5. Add the lid and cook on low heat 8-9 hours, or on high 4 ½ hours, or until pork and vegetables are tender.
6. transfer pork and vegetables to a serving plate and keep warm.
7. In a small saucepan, over medium heat, whisk together the cornstarch and water until smooth.
8. Add the liquid from the crock pot and cook, stirring, until sauce is bubbling and thick, about 4-5 minutes.
9. top pork and vegetables with sauce and serve the orzo on the side.

Nutrition Facts:Per Serving: Calories 471, total Carbs 16g, net Carbs 13g, Fiber 3g, Protein 51g, Fat 21g, saturated Fat 7g, sugar 5g, sodium 352mg, Cholesterol 159mg

Succulent Pork Chops And Beans

Servings: 2
Cooking Time: 8 Hours
Ingredients:
- 4 Pork Cutlets, pounded down to 1/4in
- ½ a cup of drained and rinsed Cannellini Beans
- ¼ of a cup of pitted and halved Kalamata Olives
- ¼ of a cup of Parsley Leaves
- 1 medium thinly sliced Capsicum
- 1 large thinly sliced Spring onions
- ½ a tbsp of Red Wine Vinegar
- 1 tbsp of Olive Oil
- Sea Salt to taste
- Freshly cracked Black Pepper to taste

Directions:
1. Season the pork on both sides with the salt and pepper, then place it in your cockpot with the rest of the Ingredients:
2. Cook, covered, for 5 hours on high or low for 8 hours

Nutrition Facts:Per Serving:471 cal, 16g total fat, 3.1g sat fat, 124mg chol, 123mg Sodium, 30.4g carb, 12.2g fiber, 56g protein

Italian Meatloaf

Servings: 6
Cooking Time: 5 Hours
Ingredients:
- nonstick cooking spray
- 1/3 cup tomato sauce
- ¼ tsp oregano
- ¼ tsp basil
- ¼ tsp garlic powder
- 1 lb. lean ground beef
- ½ lb. ground pork
- ¾ cup green bell pepper, chopped
- ½ cup onion, chopped
- 2/3 cup oats
- 2 eggs
- 1/8 tsp salt
- ½ cup mozzarella cheese, grated

Directions:
1. spray the crock pot with cooking spray.
2. In a small bowl, whisk together tomato sauce, oregano, basil, and garlic powder.
3. In a large bowl, combine beef, pork, bell pepper, onion, oats, eggs, tablespoons tomato sauce mixture and salt. Form mixture into a loaf shape.
4. take a sheet of foil, long enough to cover the bottom and sides of the crock pot and fold it in half, then half again. Lay it in the crock pot and spray with cooking spray.
5. Place the meatloaf on the foil sling. spread the remaining tomato sauce mixture over the top.
6. Add the lid and cook on low heat 5 hours, or on high 2 ½ hours, or until meatloaf is cooked through.
7. top with mozzarella cheese and cook just until it melts. Remove the lid and let sit 15 minutes.
8. Use the foil to lift the meatloaf out of the crock pot, slice and serve.

Nutrition Facts:Per Serving: Calories 418, total Carbs 14g, net Carbs 11g, Fiber 3g, Protein 26g, Fat 28g, saturated Fat 10g, sugar 1g, sodium 276mg, Cholesterol 86mg

Pork And Pumpkin Stew

Servings:8
Cooking Time: 4 Hours
Ingredients:

- 16 oz fat trimmed pork shoulder, 1-inch cubes
- 1/ tbsp salt-free seasoning
- 1 cup low-sodium beef broth
- 1 peeled and seeded pie pumpkin
- 4 fresh thyme sprigs
- 1 tbsp olive oil
- 2 tbsp tomato paste
- ¼ tbsp ground cinnamon
- ½ tbsp black pepper
- 1 large peeled onion
- 4 large diced celery stalks
- 3 large peeled carrots
- 4 minced garlic cloves
- 1 bay leaf
- 14 ounces rinsed and drained black beans

Directions:

1. Season the pork shoulder with seasoning and salt.
2. Add oil in a sauté pan and cook the seasoned pork for about 8 minutes until browned. Remove and set aside.
3. To the pan, add beef broth, tomato paste, and cinnamon, then whisk. This is to incorporate all brown bits on the pan bottom. Remove from heat.
4. Add liquid, browned pork and the remaining ingredients in a crockpot. Stir them to combine.
5. Cover and cook for about 3 hours 40 minutes on high.
6. Add beans, stir and cook for an additional 20 minutes. Remove bay leaf.
7. Serve and enjoy.

Nutrition Facts:Per Serving: Calories: 150, total fat: 4g, saturated fat: 1g, total carbs: 15g, net carbs: 10g, protein: 14g, sugars: 4g, fiber: 5g, sodium: 170mg, potassium: 640mg

Moroccan Beef Tagine

Servings: 2
Cooking Time: 9 Hours
Ingredients:

- 1/2lb Beef Chuck Roast
- 1 small Carrot, sliced in 2 inch pieces
- ½ a cup of thinly sliced Onion
- ¼ of a cup of chopped Dates
- 2 cloves of chopped Garlic
- 1 tbsp of Unsalted Ghee or Butter
- ½ a cup of fire roasted diced Tomatoes
- 1 tbsp of Raw Honey
- ½ a tbsp of Spicy Harissa Paste
- 1 tbsp of ras el hanout
- ½ a tsp of Cinnamon
- 1 cup of uncooked Couscous
- ¼ of a cup of fresh Cilantro Leaves for Garnish
- ½ a cup of Feta Cheese, crumbled for serving

Directions:

1. Oil or spray your slow cooker bowl with non-stick spray
2. Make the couscous according to the instructions on the packet, without butter or salt
3. Place all the ingredients in your crockpot and cook, covered, for 8 to 9 hours
4. When tender Shred the beef and remove any bits of fat or hard pieces
5. Stir the shredded beef back into the sauce in your crockpot
6. Serve the Tagine spooned over the couscous and sprinkled with cilantro and the feta cheese

Nutrition Facts:Per Serving:340 cal, 11g total fat, 4.5 sat fat, 55mg chol, 890g sodium, 3g carb, 3g fiber, 22g protein

Mexican Meatloaf

Servings:8
Cooking Time: 4 Hours
Ingredients:

- 2 tbsp Worcestershire sauce
- 12 crushed saltines
- ⅛ tbsp cayenne pepper
- 2 pounds lean beef, ground
- 6 tbsp divided ketchup
- 1 tbsp paprika
- 6 minced garlic cloves
- ½ tbsp pepper
- ½ tbsp salt

Directions:

1. Cut three heavy-duty foil into 20x3-inch, then crisscross to resemble wheel spokes. Place them in a crockpot, 3-qt, on the sides and the bottom. Use cooking spray to coat the strips.
2. Combine sauce, tbsp ketchup, onion, saltines, paprika, garlic, pepper, salt, and cayenne in a bowl, large.
3. Now break the beef and mix well over the mixture.
4. Shape the mixture into a round loaf then place on the strips at the center.
5. Cover the crockpot and cook for about 4-hours on low until no pink is seen.
6. Transfer the meatloaf to a platter. Use the strips as handles.
7. Sprinkle the remaining ketchup over the meatloaf.
8. Serve and enjoy.

Nutrition Facts:Per Serving: Calories: 222, total fat: 10g, saturated fat: 4g, total carbs: 10g, net carbs: , protein: 23g, sugars: 5g, fiber: 1g, sodium: 447mg, potassium: 235mg

Balsamic Brisket With Caramelized Onions

Servings: 10
Cooking Time: 8 Hours
Ingredients:
- 3 tbsp. olive oil, divided
- 4 cups onions, sliced
- 4 cloves garlic, diced fine
- 1 tbsp. brown sugar
- 4-5 lb. beef brisket, cut in half
- 1/3 cup flour
- 1 tsp salt
- 1 tsp pepper
- ¼ cup balsamic vinegar
- 14 ½ oz. beef broth, low sodium
- 2 tbsp. tomato paste
- 2 tsp Italian seasoning
- 1 tsp Worcestershire sauce
- ½ tsp paprika
- 1 tbsp. cornstarch
- 2 tbsp. water

Directions:
1. Heat tablespoon oil in a large skillet over medium heat.
2. Add onions and cook, occasionally stirring, until soft. Add garlic and brown sugar, reduce heat to med-low and cook until onions are golden brown. transfer to crock pot.
3. Place flour in a shallow dish. Coat both sides of the brisket halves and shake off excess.
4. Add remaining oil to the skillet and brown both sides of the brisket piece. sprinkle with salt and pepper and add to the crock pot.
5. Add the vinegar to the skillet and increase heat to med-high. Cook, stirring to scrape up browned bits from the bottom of the pan.
6. stir in broth, tomato paste, Italian seasoning, Worcestershire, and paprika until combined. Pour over brisket.
7. Add the lid and cook on low heat 8-10 hours until beef is tender.
8. Remove brisket to a serving plate and keep warm. Pour the cooking liquid in a saucepan and skim off the fat.
9. Bring to a boil. In a small bowl, whisk together cornstarch and water until smooth and stir into saucepan. Return to boil and cook, stirring, until thickened.
10. Cut brisket across the grain in thin slices and serve with sauce.

Nutrition Facts:Per Serving: Calories 395, total Carbs 12g, net Carbs , Fiber 1g, Protein 51g, Fat 16g, saturated Fat 5g, sugar 4g, sodium 445mg, Cholesterol 152mg

Beef Provencal

Servings: 8
Cooking Time: 5 Hours
Ingredients:

- 2 tsp olive oil
- 2 lb. beef chuck roast, boneless, cut in 1-inch cubes
- 1 ½ tsp salt, divided
- ½ tsp pepper, divided
- 2 cups carrots, chopped
- 1 ½ cups onion, chopped
- 12 cloves garlic, crushed
- 1 tbsp. tomato paste
- 1 cup dry red wine
- 14 ½ oz. tomatoes, diced
- ½ cup beef broth, low sodium
- 1 tsp fresh rosemary, chopped
- 1 tsp fresh thyme, chopped
- 1 bay leaf
- 1/8 tsp cloves

Directions:

1. Heat oil in a large skillet over med-high heat.
2. sprinkle beef with ½ teaspoon salt and ¼ teaspoon pepper. Add to skillet and cook until brown on the outside. transfer beef to the crock pot.
3. Add carrot, onion, and remaining salt and pepper to the skillet. Cook, frequently stirring, until golden brown, about 4-6 minutes.
4. stir in tomato paste and cook 1 minute more. Add wine and stir to loosen up brown bits from the bottom of the pan. Bring to a boil.
5. Add the tomatoes, broth, and seasonings to the crock pot. Pour in the wine mixture and stir to combine.
6. Add the lid and cook on low heat 5-7 hours until beef is tender. discard the bay leaf and serve.

Nutrition Facts:Per Serving: Calories 282, total Carbs 10g, net Carbs 8g, Fiber 2g, Protein 32g, Fat 11g, saturated Fat 4g, sugar 4g, sodium 608mg, Cholesterol 94mg

Pork Pot Roast With Tangerines

Servings: 2
Cooking Time: 8 Hours
Ingredients:
- 1/2lb of Rolled Pork Loin
- 2 segmented Tangerines
- 1 small sliced Onion
- 1 small finely diced Onion
- 1 clove of finely diced Garlic
- 1 sticks of finely diced Celery
- 1 tbsp of finely chopped fresh Oregano
- 1 finely diced Bacon Rasher
- 1 tsp of Cashew Flour

Directions:
1. Mix together the bacon, diced onion, celery, garlic and oregano and rub it all over the pork
2. Place the sliced onion evenly on the bottom of your crockpot and place the pork on top with the tangerine around the sides
3. Cook, covered, on low for 7 to 8 hours
4. 15 minutes before you want to serve the pork, remove it from the slow cooker and set it aside
5. Thicken the juices in the slow cooker with the cashew flour
6. Slice the pork and serve it with the sauce made from the juices

Nutrition Facts:Per Serving: Cal 101, Total fat 4.9g, chol 11g, soduim 230mg, Carb10,2g, fiber 1. Protein 4.9g

Flank Steak Tacos

Servings:12
Cooking Time: 6 Hours
Ingredients:
- 1¼ lb flank steak
- 1 juiced lime
- ¾ cup Pico de Gallo
- 12, 6-inch corn tortillas
- 1 tbsp garlic powder
- 2 tbsp chili powder
- 1 tbsp cumin
- ½ cup water

Directions:
1. Place the steak in a crockpot then splash with garlic powder, chili powder, and cumin.
2. Pour lime juice over the steak then water.
3. Cover the crockpot and cook for about 6 hours on low until done.
4. Shred using a fork then scoop 1½ ounces to each tortilla.
5. Top 1 tbsp Pico de Gallo to each taco.
6. Enjoy.

Nutrition Facts:Per Serving: Calories: 130, total fat: 4g, saturated fat: 1.5g, total carbs: 13g, net carbs: 11g, protein: 11g, sugars: 1g, fiber: 2g, sodium: 110mg, potassium: 240mg

African Beef Stew

Servings: 6
Cooking Time: 7 Hours
Ingredients:

- 3 tbsp. flour
- 1 ½ tbsp. extra virgin olive oil
- 1 ½ lbs. chuck roast, cubed
- 1 tsp salt
- 1 tsp black pepper
- 3 cloves garlic, diced fine
- ¼ tsp ginger
- ¼ tsp crushed red pepper flakes
- 1 tsp cumin
- 1 tsp paprika
- 1 tsp ground coriander
- ¼ tsp turmeric
- 1 onion, chopped
- 2 carrots, sliced
- 2 stalks celery, sliced
- 15 oz. tomatoes, diced
- 1 ½ cups beef broth, low sodium
- ¼ cup almonds, sliced
- 1 cup golden raisins

Directions:

1. Place flour in a shallow bowl.
2. Heat oil in a large skillet over medium heat.
3. Coat beef cubes with flour, shaking off excess, and add to skillet. Cook until brown on the outside, about 5 minutes. transfer to the crock pot, with the drippings in the pan.
4. Add remaining ingredients, except almonds and raisins and stir to mix.
5. Add the lid and cook on low heat 6-8 hours or on high 4-6 hours until beef and vegetables are tender.
6. stir in almonds and raisins and cook on high 10 minutes. serve.

Nutrition Facts:Per Serving: Calories 339, total Carbs 32g, net Carbs 2, Fiber 5g, Protein 29g, Fat 12g, saturated Fat 3g, sugar 19g, sodium 558mg, Cholesterol 73mg

Beef Salsa With Squash Noodles And Tomatoes

Servings: 2
Cooking Time: 5 Hours
Ingredients:

- 1/2lb of lean Ground Beef
- ½ a cup of crushed Tomatoes
- 1 small finely diced Onion
- 2 tsp of crushed Garlic
- 1 fresh Bay Leaf
- 1 tbsp of finely chopped Sun-Dried Tomatoes
- 2 tbsp of Roasted Red Pepper Flakes
- Sea Salt to taste
- Fresh ground Black Pepper to taste
- Chili powder to taste

Directions:

1. Place all the ingredients except the squash noodles in your crockpot and mix to combine evenly, then cook covered on high for 5 hours, Steam the squash noodles lightly and serve with the salsa

Nutrition Facts:Per Serving: Cal 150, Total fat 3g, Sat fat 1g, Chol 35mg, Sodium 660mg, Carb 16g, fiber 5g Protein 16g

Swiss Steak

Servings: 4
Cooking Time: 6 Hours

Ingredients:
- 1 onion, sliced
- 1 carrot, sliced
- 2 tbsp. extra virgin olive oil
- 4 top round steaks
- 1 tsp salt
- ½ tsp pepper
- ½ cup flour
- 1 cup mushrooms, sliced
- ¾ cup beef broth, low sodium
- ¼ cup tomato sauce
- 1 tsp thyme
- 1 tsp paprika
- ½ cup Greek yogurt
- 2 tbsp. fresh parsley, chopped

Directions:
1. Place the onion and carrots in the crock pot.
2. Heat the oil in a large skillet over medium heat.
3. sprinkle both sides of the steaks with salt and pepper.
4. Place the flour in a shallow dish and dredge the steaks, coating both sides.
5. Cook steaks in the hot oil until brown on both sides. transfer to the crock pot.
6. Place mushrooms on top of steaks.
7. Add the broth to the skillet and whisk, scraping up brown bits. stir in tomato sauce, thyme, and paprika and pour over ingredients in the crock pot.
8. Add the lid and cook on low heat 6-hours, or on high 4-5 hours until steaks and vegetables are tender.
9. transfer steaks to a serving plate. stir the yogurt and parsley into cooking liquid and cook 10 minutes, or until heated through. Ladle sauce over steaks and serve.

Nutrition Facts:Per Serving: Calories 483, total Carbs 23g, net Carbs 21g, Fiber 2g, Protein 43g, Fat 23g, saturated Fat 8g, sugar 6g, sodium 915mg, Cholesterol 122mg

Delightful Burgundy Lamb Shanks

Servings: 2
Cooking Time: 8 Hours
Ingredients:
- 2 Lamb Shanks (20 oz each)
- 1 cup of a nice drinking Burgundy
- 1 small chopped Onion
- 1 small chopped Carrot
- 1 tsp of dried Parsley
- 1 tbsp of minced Garlic
- ½ of a tsp of dried Oregano'
- ½ a tsp of grated Lemon Peel
- 1/8 of a tsp of ground Cloves
- 1 Bay Leaf
- A Sprig of Rosemary
- A Sprig of Thyme
- 1 tsp of Olive Oil
- Sea Salt to taste
- Ground Black Pepper to taste

Directions:
1. Place everything in your crockpot and cook covered on low for 8 hours
2. Take the juices from your crockpot and strain, then reduce them to a nice sauce consistency in a small saucepan
3. Serve the Lamb Shanks with the gravy and a fresh salad

Nutrition Facts:Per Serving: Cal 633, fat 27g, sat fat 13g, carb 6g, chol 228mg, sodium 4mg, fiber 1g, protein 69g

Healthy Hamburger Casserole

Servings: 8
Cooking Time: 4 Hours
Ingredients:
- nonstick cooking spray
- 1 lb. lean ground beef
- ½ cup red bell pepper, chopped
- 8 oz. mushrooms, sliced
- 2 (8 oz) cans tomato sauce, no salt added
- 1 tsp garlic powder
- ½ tsp black pepper
- 3 cups no-yolk egg noodles, uncooked
- 6 oz. cream cheese, reduced-fat, soft
- 1/3 cup sour cream, reduced-fat
- 2 green onions, sliced
- ¼ cup cheddar cheese, grated

Directions:
1. spray the crock pot with cooking spray.
2. In a large skillet, over medium heat, cook the beef, bell pepper, and mushrooms until beef is no longer pink. drain off fat.
3. stir in tomato sauce, seasonings, and noodles.
4. In a medium bowl, beat together cream cheese and sour cream until smooth. stir in half the green onion.
5. spoon half the beef mixture into the crock pot. top with cheese mixture then remaining beef mixture.
6. Add the lid and cook on low heat 4 hours, or on high 2 hours.
7. sprinkle the cheese over the top and cook until it melts.
8. Garnish with remaining green onions and serve.

Nutrition Facts:Per Serving: Calories 250, total Carbs 24g, net Carbs 22g, Fiber 2g, Protein 20g, Fat , saturated Fat 5g, sugar 6g, sodium 170mg, Cholesterol 51mg

Chipotle Steak Simmer

Servings: 6
Cooking Time: 2 Hours
Ingredients:
- 1½ lb top round roast, cubed
- ½ tbsp Mexican seasoning, salt-free
- ½ tbsp Adobo sauce, from the chipotle pepper can
- 1tbsp Worcestershire sauce
- 2 cups canned tomatoes, crushed
- ¼ tbsp kosher salt
- 2 finely chopped chipotle peppers, from the can
- 1 tbsp brown sugar
- 3 tbsp olive oil
- 1½ cup red onion, 1-inch squares
- 1 tbsp finely minced garlic
- 1½ cup poblano pepper, 1-inch squares

Directions:
1. Place the roast into a bowl then season with salt and the seasoning. Mix to evenly coat and set aside.
2. Place finely chopped chipotle peppers to a bowl then add ½ tbsp adobo sauce, Worcestershire sauce, crushed tomatoes, and brown sugar. Mix to combine and set aside.
3. Add 1 tbsp olive to a hot nonstick skillet over medium heat. Add onion, garlic, and poblano peppers then spread to an even layer. Cook while occasionally stirring until crisp-tender and cooked evenly.
4. Transfer to a crockpot and return pan to heat.
5. Add 1 tbsp oil to the pan distributing evenly over the pan, then add half of seasoned roast cubes. Cook for about 1 minute on each side until browned.
6. Add the roast to the pot then stir in adobo and tomato mixture. Make sure the roast is submerged.
7. Cover the pot and cook for about 2-4 hours on low until the roast pulls apart easily with a fork.
8. Serve immediately and enjoy it.
Nutrition Facts:Per Serving: Calories: 1, total fat: 6g, saturated fat: 2g, total carbs: 13g, net carbs: 11g, Protein: 26g, sugars: 7g, Fiber: 2g, sodium: 390mg, potassium: 570mg

Quinoa Enchilada Bake

Servings: 2
Cooking Time: 4 Hours
Ingredients:
- ½lb of lean ground Beef
- 1 small diced Green Capsicum
- 1 small diced Onion
- 1 clove of minced Garlic
- ¼ of a cup of Quinoa
- ½ a cup of cooked Black Beans
- ¼ of a cup of cooked Yellow Corn
- 1 cup of Vegetable Stock or Broth
- ½ a cup of diced Tomatoes with Green Chilies
- ½ a cup of Tomato Sauce
- 1 tbsp of Chili Powder or to taste
- 1 tsp of Cumin

Directions:
1. Place everything except the black beans and corn in your crockpot and stir to evenly mix, then cook covered on high for 3.75 hours, then add the beans and corn and cook minutes more
2. Serve over chopped green leafy vegetables or in a corn tortilla
Nutrition Facts:Per Serving: Cal 150g, Fat 5g, Sodium 280mg, Carb15g Fiber , Protein 13g

Spanish Meatballs

Servings: 2
Cooking Time: 8 Hours
Ingredients:
- 1/2lb of ground Pork (or beef if preferred)
- 1 small finely chopped Onion
- ½ a cup of diced tomatoes
- 1 large beaten lightly Egg
- 1 tbsp of finely chopped fresh Parsley
- 1 tsp of ground Black Cumin
- 1 ½ tsp of Hot Smoked Paprika
- ½ a cup of Breadcrumbs
- 1 tbsp of Olive Oil
- Sea Salt to taste
- Freshly ground Black Pepper to taste

Directions:
1. Oil your crockpot
2. Place half the tomatoes and onions and all the rest of the ingredients in a bowl and mix them thoroughly together
3. Form the mixture into balls about 1 ½ inches across, you should get 12 balls
4. Place the meatballs in your crockpot with the rest of the onion and tomatoes to make a sauce
5. Cook, covered, on low for hours and serve

Nutrition Facts:Per Serving:524 calories, 21.8g total fat, 259mg chol, 329mg sodium, 14. carb, 2.1g fiber, 65.1g protein

Pork Stew

Servings:8
Cooking Time: 5 Hours
Ingredients:
- 2 pound pork tenderloins, 2-inch pieces
- 2 carrots, ½ -inch slices
- 2 coarsely chopped celery ribs
- 1 fresh thyme sprig
- 1 fresh rosemary sprig
- ½ tbsp pepper
- 1 tbsp salt
- 1 coarsely chopped onion, medium
- 2 tbsp tomato paste
- 3 cups beef broth
- 4 minced garlic cloves
- ⅓ Cup pitted and chopped plums, dried
- 2 bay leaves

Directions:
1. Splash pepper and salt on the pork and transfer to a crockpot.
2. Add carrots, onion, and celery.
3. Meanwhile, whisk tomato paste, and beef broth in a bowl then pour over the vegetables.
4. Add garlic, plums, bay leaves, thyme, and rosemary.
5. Cover the crockpot and cook for about 6 hours on low until vegetables and pork are tender.
6. Discard thyme, bay leaves, and rosemary.
7. Serve with potatoes. Enjoy!

Nutrition Facts:Per Serving: Calories: 177, total fat: 4g, saturated fat: 1g, total carbs: 9g, Net carbs: , Protein: 24g, sugars: 4g, Fiber: 1g, sodium: 64mg, potassium: 99mg

Tender Sunday Roast Beef

Servings: 2
Cooking Time: 7 Hours
Ingredients:
- 1/2lb of Boneless Beef Chuck Roast
- ½ a cup of chopped Onion
- 1 clove of minced Garlic
- 1 tsp of Italian seasoning
- 1 tsp of Onion Powder
- ½ a tsp of Sea Salt
- ½ a tsp of Black Pepper
- ¼ of a cup of Red Wine or Red Wine Vinegar
- ½ a cup of diced Tomatoes

Directions:
1. Place everything in your crockpot and cook, covered, on low for 8 to 9 hours

Nutrition Facts:Per Serving: Cal 1, Fat 3.2g, chol, 72mg, sodium 267mg, Protein 16g

Lamb And Aubergine Casserole

Servings: 2
Cooking Time: 8 Hours
Ingredients:
- ½lb of Lamb Meat
- ½ a cup of diced Tomatoes
- ½ a cup of Beef Stock or Broth
- 1 small diced Onion
- 1 medium diced Carrots
- ¼ of a cup of dried Apricots
- 1 clove of minced Garlic
- 1 tsp of dried crushed Oregano
- 1 tsp of ground Turmeric
- ¼ of a tsp of ground Cinnamon
- 1 cup of Aubergine, cut in 1 inch cubes
- 2 tbsp of chopped Fresh Parsley

Directions:
1. Place everything except the aubergine in your crockpot and cook, covered, on high for 5 hours
2. Add the eggplant and cook, covered, 30 minutes longer and add the parsley just before serving

Nutrition Facts:Per Serving: Cal249, total fat 10g, sat fat , chol 11mg, sodium 513, Carb 27g, fiber 8g, protein 39g

Slow-cooked Flank Steak

Servings:6
Cooking Time: 4 Hours
Ingredients:
- 1 tbsp canola oil
- 1½ pounds flank steak
- 4 ounces green chilies, chopped
- 1¼ tbsp chili powder
- 1 tbsp garlic powder
- 1 sliced onion, large
- ⅓ Cup water
- 2 tbsp vinegar
- ½ tbsp sugar
- ½ tbsp salt
- ⅛ tbsp pepper

Directions:
1. Pour the oil in a skillet, then add steak and cook until brown. Transfer to a crockpot.
2. Now sauté the onion in the skillet for about 1 minute.
3. Add water gradually while stirring. This is to loosen brown bits out of the pan.
4. Add the rest of the ingredients then boil.
5. Pour over the browned steak.
6. Cover the crockpot then cook for about 4-5 hours on low until the steak is tender.
7. Slice the flank steak.
8. Serve with pan juices and onion.

Nutrition Facts:Per Serving: Calories: 1, total fat: 11g, saturated fat: 4g, total carbs: 4g, net carbs: 3g, protein: 20g, sugars: 3g, fiber: 1g, sodium: 327mg, potassium: 756mg

Meat Loaf Supreme

Servings:2
Cooking Time: 8 Hours
Ingredients:
- ½lb of Ground Beef, Mutton or Pork
- ¼ of a cup of finely diced Sun-dried Tomatoes
- 1 clove of crushed Garlic
- 1 lightly beaten Egg
- 1 tbsp of Milk
- ¼ of a cup of Feta Cheese
- 1oz of Green Olives
- ¼ a cup of Breadcrumbs
- ¼ of a tsp of dried Oregano crushed
- ¼ of a tsp of Ground Black Pepper
- ¼ of a cup of Pasta Sauce

Directions:
1. Combine together the milk, eggs, oregano, pepper, garlic, tomatoes and breadcrumbs. Then add in the feta cheese and ground meat, mix everything well
2. Then place the mixture into a dish that will fit inside your crockpot and accommodate the meatloaf and sauce
3. Place the bowl in your crockpot and pour the pasta sauce over the meat loaf
4. Cook it covered for hours on high or 7 to 8 hours on low

Nutrition Facts:Per Serving:238 cal, 9g total fat, 4g sat fat, 74mg chol, 324mg sodium, 10g carb, 1g fiber, 29g protein 12

White Beans & Bacon

Servings: 8
Cooking Time: 8 Hours
Ingredients:
- 4 cups white beans, soak overnight, rinse & drain
- 2 ½ cups chicken broth, low sodium
- 2 tbsp. red wine vinegar
- 4 cloves garlic, diced fine
- 1 ½ tbsp. fresh basil, chopped
- 1 ½ tbsp. fresh rosemary, chopped
- 3 tbsp. fresh parsley, chopped
- ½ tsp red pepper flakes
- ½ tsp salt
- ½ tsp black pepper
- 2 cups water
- 8 slices bacon, chopped

Directions:
1. Add the beans, broth, vinegar, garlic, seasonings, and water to the crock pot. stir to mix.
2. Add the lid and cook on low heat 8 hours, or until beans are tender.
3. Heat a skillet over med-high heat and cook the bacon until crisp. transfer to a paper towel-lined plate.
4. When the beans are tender, stir in the bacon and serve.

Nutrition Facts:Per Serving: Calories 248, total Carbs 2, net Carbs 20g, Fiber 5g, Protein 13g, Fat 11g, saturated Fat 0g, sugar 1g, sodium 297mg, Cholesterol 0mg

Tantalizing Goat Curry

Servings:2
Cooking Time: 5 Hours
Ingredients:
- ½lb of diced Goat Meat
- 1 small chopped Red Onion
- ½ a tsp of minced fresh Ginger
- 1 clove of minced Garlic
- 1 tsp of Ghee or Coconut Oil
- 1 Bay Leaf
- A pinch of ground Cloves
- A pinch of ground Cardamom
- A pinch of ground Cayenne
- 1 tsp of ground Coriander
- ¼ of a tsp of ground Cumin
- ½ a tsp of ground Turmeric
- ½ a tsp of ground Paprika
- ½ a cup of diced Tomatoes
- ¼ of a tsp of Gram Masala (or chili powder)
- Water as needed

Directions:
1. Combine and thoroughly mix everything except the diced tomatoes and gram masala
2. Cook, covered, on high for 4 hours, then add the tomatoes and gram masala, plus a little water it the curry is too thick. Continue cooking until the meat is tender

Nutrition Facts:Per Serving: Cal 169, Total fat 5g, sat fat 2.7g, chol 57mg, sodium 91mg, Carb 8.6g, fiber 2.2g, protein 22.7g

Mandarin Beef

Servings: 6
Cooking Time: 8 Hours
Ingredients:
- 1 lb. beef chuck blade steak, boneless & cut in bite-size pieces
- ½ tsp salt
- ½ tsp black pepper
- 1 carrot, diced
- 1 onion, diced
- 1 red bell pepper, cut in strips
- 2 cloves garlic, diced fine
- 1 tsp fresh ginger, grated
- 1 tsp sesame oil
- 1 tbsp. rice vinegar
- 1 tbsp. soy sauce, low sodium
- 1 can mandarin oranges
- 2 tbsp. cornstarch

Directions:
1. sprinkle beef with salt and pepper and place in crock pot.
2. Add remaining ingredients, except for oranges and cornstarch. stir to combine.
3. Add the lid and cook on low heat 6-8 hours, or until beef is tender.
4. 15 minutes before cooking time ends, whisk the cornstarch and ¼ cup liquid from the oranges together until smooth.
5. stir into the beef mixture until combined. Add the oranges. Continue cooking 1minutes or until the mixture thickens. stir well and serve.

Nutrition Facts:Per Serving: Calories 23 total Carbs 10g, net Carbs 9g, Fiber 1g, Protein 16g, Fat 15g, saturated Fat 6g, sugar 6g, sodium 220mg, Cholesterol 69mg

Cauliflower & Bacon Soup

Servings: 4
Cooking Time: 5 Hours
Ingredients:
- 1 head cauliflower, chopped
- 3 cloves garlic, diced fine
- 1 onion, chopped
- 4 cups vegetable broth, low sodium
- 4 slices turkey bacon, chopped & cooked crisp

Directions:
1. Combine the cauliflower, garlic, onion, and broth in the crock pot.
2. Add the lid and cook on low heat 5 hours, or on high 3 hours.
3. Use an immersion blender and process soup until almost smooth.
4. Ladle into bowls and top with bacon, serve.

Nutrition Facts:Per Serving: Calories 173, total Carbs 11g, net Carbs 8g, Fiber 3g, Protein 7g, Fat 12g, saturated Fat 4g, sugar 4g, sodium 270mg, Cholesterol 19mg

Taco Casserole

Servings: 6
Cooking Time: 4 Hours
Ingredients:
- nonstick cooking spray
- 1 lb. lean ground beef
- ¼ cup onion, chopped
- 1 jalapeno, diced fine
- 1 packet taco seasoning
- ¼ cup water
- 2 oz. cream cheese
- ¼ cup salsa
- 4 eggs
- 1 tbsp. hot sauce
- ¼ cup heavy whipping cream
- ½ cup cheddar cheese, grated
- ½ cup pepper jack cheese, grated

Directions:
1. spray the crock pot with cooking spray.
2. In a large skillet, over medium heat, cook ground beef until no longer pink.
3. Add the onion and jalapeno and cook until onion is translucent. drain off the fat.
4. stir in the taco seasoning and water and simmer 5 minutes, or until most of the liquid is evaporated.
5. stir in the cream cheese and salsa and transfer to the crock pot.
6. In a medium bowl, whisk together eggs, hot sauce, and cream. Pour over the beef mixture.
7. sprinkle both cheeses over the top. Add the lid and cook on low heat 4 hours, or on high 2 hours until eggs are set and casserole is bubbly. Let cool 5 minutes before serving.

Nutrition Facts:Per Serving: Calories 355, total Carbs 4g, net Carbs 3g, Fiber 1g, Protein 30g, Fat 23g, saturated Fat 11g, sugar 2g, sodium 554mg, Cholesterol 22g

Shredded Green Chili Beef

Servings:12
Cooking Time: 7 Hours
Ingredients:
- 4 tbsp brown sugar, packed and divided
- 1 tbsp paprika
- 3 pounds beef chuck roast, boneless
- 28 ounces green enchilada sauce
- 2 thinly sliced and halved sweet onions, large
- 1½ tbsp salt
- 1 tbsp cayenne pepper
- 1tbsp chili powder
- 1 tbsp garlic powder
- ½ tbsp pepper
- 2 tbsp canola oil

Directions:
1. Place 3tbsp sugar and onions in a crockpot, 5-qt or 6-qt.
2. In the meantime, combine 1 tbsp sugar, paprika, salt, cayenne pepper, chili powder, garlic powder, and pepper in a mixing bowl.
3. Marinate the beef with the mixture.
4. Now heat the oil in a skillet, large, and brown the beef for about 1-2 minutes over high-medium heat on each side.
5. Transfer the beef to a crockpot and pour the sauce over.
6. Cover the crockpot and cook for about 7-9 hours on low until beef is tender.
7. Remove from the pot then shred using two forks.
8. Return to the pot to heat through.
9. Serve with potatoes if desired.

Nutrition Facts:Per Serving: Calories: 278, total fat: 15g, saturated fat: 4g, total carbs: 14g, net carbs: 13g, Protein: 23g, sugars: 8g, Fiber: 1g, sodium: 658mg, potassium: 743mg

Desserts and Snacks

Popcorns

Servings:4
Cooking Time: 30 Minutes
Ingredients:
- 4 tbsp coconut oil
- 1 cup Safeway popcorn
- 4 tbsp butter
- ¼ Himalayan salt

Directions:
1. Add coconut oil in your crockpot and swirl it so that the bottom is well covered. Heat the crockpot until the oil sizzles.
2. Add the popcorn and use a wooden spatula to coat them well with oil.
3. Cover with a clear lid so that you will see when most of the popcorn has popped.
4. Turn off the heat and remove the lid. Pour the popcorn into a bowl and let it rest for two minutes.
5. Add butter and salt to taste. Serve and enjoy.

Nutrition Facts:Per Serving: Calories 18 Total Fat 13g, Saturated Fat 9g, Total Carbs 14g, Net Carbs 12g, Protein 2g, Sugar 3g, Fiber 2g, Sodium 124mg, Potassium 56 mg

Amazing Carrot Cake

Servings:2
Cooking Time: 3 Hours
Ingredients:
- ¾ of a cup of Unsweetened Applesauce
- 2 very ripe Bananas
- 1 large egg, at room temperature
- 1/2 a cup of Flour
- 1 tsp of Baking Soda
- 1½ tsp of Baking Powder
- ½ a tsp of Sea Salt
- 1 tsp of Ground Cinnamon
- 2 cups of Grated Carrots
- ½ a cup of Shredded Coconut
- ½ a cup of Chopped Nuts of your choice
- ½ a tsp of Pure Vanilla Extract
- ½ a cup of unsweetened Crushed Pineapple, with juice
- 2 tbsp of Unsalted Butter (softened)
- 4oz of Cream Cheese (softened)
- 1 tsp of Pure Vanilla Extract
- ¼ of a cup of Powered Erythritol

Directions:
1. Oil a cake tin that will fit inside your crockpot
2. Whisk together the eggs, sugar and applesauce with the baking powder, baking soda, flour, cinnamon and salt
3. Stir in the carrots, nuts, coconut, pineapple and vanilla extract
4. Gently pour the batter into the cake tin and place in your crockpot
5. Place three folded paper towels over the top of the slow cooker
6. Cook, covered, on low for 3 hours the check using a toothpick inserted in the center
7. Allow the cake cool completely before frosting
8. Cream Cheese Frosting
9. Beat the cream cheese and butter together until it's fluffy
10. Add in the powered Erythritol and vanilla, then beat it until it becomes nice and smooth
11. Frost the cake when it's completely cooled, cutting into the layers if desired
12. Top with toasted coconut

Nutrition Facts:Per Serving: Cal 460, total fat 16.6g, chol 8.6g, sodium 200mg, carb 75.1g, fiber 2.3g, protein 5.7g

Skinny Pecan Pie

Servings: 16
Cooking Time: 4 Hours
Ingredients:
- nonstick cooking spray
- 1 (9-inch) whole wheat pie crust
- 1/2 cup honey for a mildly sweet pie OR 3/4 cup honey for a moderately sweet pie
- 3 egg whites, whipped with a fork
- 2 cups diced pecans
- 4 teaspoons vanilla extract
- 1 teaspoon cinnamon
- 3 tablespoons cornstarch or white whole wheat flour

Directions:
1. spray the crock pot with cooking spray. Line the bottom with a piece of parchment paper.
2. Place the pie crust in the crock pot and mold it to fit the inside.
3. In a large bowl, beat together all the ingredients until well combined.
4. Pour the filling into the crust. Use a knife to carefully cut away the excess crust at the top.
5. Place two sheets of paper towels over the top of the crock pot and add the lid. Cook on low heat 3 hours.
6. Remove the lid and the paper towels and continue cooking, without the lid, for another minutes.
7. Carefully use a knife to loosen the pie around the edges. Once the pie is loose, carefully remove the pie and transfer to a serving plate to cool completely.

Nutrition Facts:Per Serving: Calories 205, total Carbs 20g, net Carbs 17g, Fiber 3g, Protein 4g, Fat 14g, saturated Fat 1g, sugar 9g, sodium mg, Cholesterol 0mg

Crockpot Sugar-free Chocolate Molten Lava Cake

Servings:12
Cooking Time: 3 Hours
Ingredients:
- 1 ½ Cup swerve sweetener, divided
- ½ cup flour, gluten-free
- 5 tbsp cocoa powder, unsweetened and divided
- 4 oz chocolate chips, sugar-free
- ½ tbsp salt
- 1 tbsp baking powder
- ½ cup butter, melted and cooled
- 3 eggs
- 3 egg yolks
- ½ tbsp vanilla liquid stevia
- 1 tbsp vanilla extract
- 2 cups hot water

Directions:
1. Grease your crockpot with cooking spray.
2. Whisk together one and a half cup swerve sweetener, flour, three tablespoon cocoa, baking powder, and salt.
3. In another mixing bowl, mix butter, eggs, egg yolks, liquid stevia, and vanilla extract.
4. Add the wet mixture to the dry mixture and mix until well combined.
5. Pour the mixture to the crockpot and top with chocolate chips.
6. Whisk together the remaining swerve sweetener and cocoa powder. Pour over the chocolate chips in the crockpot.
7. Lid the crockpot and set time for three hours. When time is done, let sit to cool.
8. Serve and enjoy.

Nutrition Facts:Per Serving: Calories 157, Total Fat 13g, Saturated Fat 6.4g, Total Carbs 10.5g, Net Carbs 7., Protein 3.9g, Sugar 0.2g, Fiber 2.6g, Sodium 166mg, Potassium 106mg

Devils Drumsticks

Servings: 2
Cooking Time: 3 To 6 Hours
Ingredients:
- Chicken Drumsticks
- ¼ of a cup of Chili Salsa
- 2 tsp of Hot Chili Sauce (more if you like it really hot)
- 1 tsp of Smoked Paprika
- ¼ of a tsp of Dried Thyme
- 1 Bay Leaf
- 2 tsp of Olive Oil

Directions:
1. Place all the ingredients in your crockpot and mix them well
2. Cook, covered, on low for 6 hours or high for 3 hours
3. Serve with the sauce in the crockpot

Nutrition Facts:Per Serving: Cal 209, total fat 9g. sat fat 2g chol98mg, sodium536mg, carb 3g, protein 27g

Delightful Peach Cobbler

Servings: 2
Cooking Time: 4 Hours
Ingredients:
- 1.1/2 cups of peeled and sliced frozen or fresh Peaches
- 1 very ripe Banana
- 1/2 a tsp of Ground Cinnamon
- 1 cup of Grahame Crackers
- 1 tbsp of Raw Sugar
- 1/2 a tsp of Ground Cinnamon
- 1/4 of a tsp of Ground Nutmeg
- 1 tsp of pure Vanilla Extract
- 1/2 a cup of Cashew Milk

Directions:
1. Insert a liner into your crockpot or spray it with non-stick spray
2. Combine the peaches, banana and cinnamon in a bowl, then spread them in your crockpot
3. Mix together the graham crackers, vanilla, sugar, nutmeg, cinnamon, and milk, stir it thoroughly until smooth
4. Spread this mixture evenly over peaches
5. Place 3 thicknesses of paper towels to stop condensation over the cobbler
6. Cook, covered, on low setting for 3-4 hours, or until set

Nutrition Facts:Per Serving: Cal 181, total fat 5.4g, sat fat, 1.5g, chol 2mg, Sodium 393mg, carb 32g, fiber 1.8g, protein 4.1g

Turkey Breasts

Servings:4
Cooking Time: 6 Hours
Ingredients:
- 1 turkey breast
- 1 tbsp garlic powder
- 1 tbsp paprika
- 1 tbsp parsley

Directions:
1. Place the turkey breast in a crockpot.
2. Season with garlic, parsley, and paprika. Let sit to marinate for five minutes.
3. Set timer for six hours. When the time elapses, remove the turkey from the crockpot and place it on a cutting board.
4. Cover with aluminum foil and let rest for ten minutes.
5. Cut into pieces and serve. Enjoy.

Nutrition Facts:Per Serving: Calories 140, Total Fat 3g, Saturated Fat 1g, Total Carbs 0g, Net Carbs 0g, Protein 27g, Sugar 0g, Fiber 0g, Sodium 41mg, Potassium 42 mg

Mozzarella Stuffed Meatballs

Servings: 6
Cooking Time: 6 Hours

Ingredients:

- 1 lb. lean ground turkey
- 1 onion, chopped fine, divided
- 1 slice whole-grain bread, lightly toasted & ground
- 1 egg
- 1 tsp salt, divided
- ½ tsp black pepper
- 3 ½ oz. ball of mozzarella, cut in small pieces
- ¼ cup whole wheat flour
- 1 ½ tbsp. extra virgin olive oil
- ½ cup chicken broth, low sodium
- 14 oz. can tomatoes, diced
- 1 tsp oregano
- 4 fresh sage leaves, chopped

Directions:

1. In a mixing bowl, combine turkey, bread crumbs, egg, half the onion, ½ teaspoons salt, and pepper.
2. Form mixture into 1-inch balls. Push a piece of the mozzarella into each ball, making sure that the cheese is completely covered.
3. Pour the flour on a shallow plate. Roll the meatballs in the flour and set aside.
4. Heat half the oil in a large skillet over medium heat. Add the meatballs and cook, stirring occasionally, until brown on the outside. transfer to a paper towel-lined bowl.
5. Add remaining oil to the skillet along with the onion and cook 3-minutes, or until onions are translucent.
6. Add the meatballs back to the skillet and pour in the broth. Cook, stirring occasionally until the sauce starts to thicken, about 5 minutes.
7. transfer the mixture to the crock pot and add remaining ingredients. stir gently to combine.
8. Add the lid and cook on low heat 6 hours, or on high 4 hours. serve warm.

Nutrition Facts:Per Serving: Calories 255, total Carbs 12g, net Carbs , Fiber 3g, Protein 21g, Fat 14g, saturated Fat 5g, sugar 3g, sodium 153mg, Cholesterol 105mg

Meatloaf On A Sling

Servings:4
Cooking Time: 5 Hours
Ingredients:
- ⅓ Cup ketchup
- 2 tbsp Worcestershire sauce
- 1 lb. beef, ground
- ⅔ Cup oats, quick-cooking
- 2 tbsp flaxseed, ground
- Nonstick cooking spray
- 1 tbsp water
- ½ cup onion, chopped
- ¾ cup green bell pepper, diced
- ½ cup egg substitute
- ⅛ tbsp salt

Directions:
1. Spray the crockpot with cooking spray.
2. Add ketchup Worcestershire sauce and water in a mixing bowl and mix.
3. In a separate bowl, combine beef, oats, flaxseed, onions, bell pepper, egg substitute salt, and three tablespoons of the ketchup mixture. Store the remaining ketchup in a fridge.
4. Lengthwise, fold paper foil sheets into half. Coat the strips with cooking spray then crisscross them in spoke like way. They will act as a sling.
5. Now place the meatloaf mixture at the center of the spokes.
6. Transfer the leaf to the crockpot, ensuring the aluminum foil in place for easy removal.
7. Cover the crockpot and cook on low for five hours.
8. Evenly apply the remaining ketchup mixture on the meatloaf and let it rest for fifteen minutes.
9. Carefully lift the foil strips to remove the meatloaf from the crockpot.
10. Serve and enjoy.

Nutrition Facts:Per Serving: Calories 259, Total Fat 7.7g, Saturated Fat 2.8g, Total Carbs 19g, Net Carbs 15g, Protein 32g, Sugar 6.5g, Fiber 3g, Sodium 409mg, Potassium 142 mg

Savory Blue Cheese Dip

Servings: 2
Cooking Time: 2 Hours
Ingredients:
- 2oz of grated Gruyere Cheese
- 3oz of Blue Cheese
- ¼ of a cup of Hot Salsa Sauce
- ¼ of a cup of finely sliced Sautéed Mushrooms
- 3 cloves of minced Garlic
- ¼ of a tsp of Ground Black Pepper

Directions:
1. Place everything in your crockpot and stir to combine, then cook, covered, on high for to 2 hours

Nutrition Facts:Per Serving: Cal 89, total fat 4g, Chol 16mg, Sodium 601mg, Carb 5g, protein 8g

Teriyaki Meatballs

Servings: 10
Cooking Time: 4 Hours
Ingredients:
- nonstick cooking spray
- 1 lb. lean ground pork
- 1/3 cup scallion, diced fine
- 1 cup light whole wheat bread crumbs
- 1/3 cup teriyaki marinade, reduced fat, divided
- ½ tsp black pepper

Directions:
1. Heat oven to broil and spray a baking sheet with cooking spray.
2. In a large bowl, combine pork, scallion, bread crumbs, tablespoons marinade, and pepper. Form into 1-inch balls and place on the prepared baking sheet. Bake 5 minutes until brown on the outside.
3. transfer the meatballs to the crock pot and pour the remaining marinade over the top. stir gently to coat.
4. Add the lid and cook on low heat hours, stirring occasionally. serve warm.

Nutrition Facts:Per Serving: Calories 1, total Carbs 7g, net Carbs 6g, Fiber 1g, Protein 10g, Fat 10g, saturated Fat 4g, sugar 2g, sodium 239mg, Cholesterol 33mg

Divine Velveeta Cheese Dip

Servings: 2
Cooking Time: 90 To 120 Minutes
Ingredients:
- 40z of Velveeta Cheese Cubed
- 1 tsp of Taco Seasoning, or to taste
- 4 minced cloves of Garlic
- ¼ of a cup of diced Tomatoes
- 2 diced Green Chili Peppers Optional

Directions:
1. Place everything in your crockpot and stir to combine, then cook, covered, for 90 to 0 minutes and serve hot or cold with tortilla or corn chips

Nutrition Facts:Per Serving: Cal 89, total fat 4g, sat fat 3g, chol 16mg, sodium, 601mg, carb 5g, protein 8g

Chocolate Chip Scones

Servings:2
Cooking Time: 3 Hours
Ingredients:
- 125g of Self Raising Flour
- A pinch of salt
- 26g of Unsalted Butter, cubed
- 15g of Caster Sugar
- 75ml of Milk, any kind
- 50 g no sugar, chocolate chips
- Any additional fillings you desire such as Sultanas, Blueberries, dried Cranberries

Directions:
1. Mix together the flour, salt and sugar in a bowl
2. Rub the butter into the flour mixture
3. Stir in the milk to form a soft dough
4. Add the chocolate chips and any other fillings you desire
5. Form the dough in a round shape that will fit into your slow cooker
6. Divide the top of the dough with a knife, making large or 12 small equal segments
7. Place a liner or oil the inside of your crockpot and place the dough inside
8. Put 3 sheets of kitchen towel right on top of your crockpot
9. Cook, covered, on high for approx 1 5 hours on high or 3 hours on low
10. Remove from the cooker and allow to cool, then slice into triangles

Nutrition Facts:Per Serving: Cal 473, total fat 17.2g, sat fat 8.8g, Chol 31mg, sodium162mg, carb 73.8g, fiber 1.7g, protein 8.9g

Cinnamon Mixed Nuts

Servings: 12
Cooking Time: 1 ½ Hours
Ingredients:
- 1 cup almonds
- 1 cup pecans
- 1 cup walnuts
- 1 ½ tsp cinnamon
- 1/3 cup honey

Directions:
1. Place the nuts in the crock pot.
2. sprinkle cinnamon over the top and add honey. stir well to make sure all the nuts are coated.
3. Add the lid and cook on low heat 1-1/2 hours. serve warm.

Nutrition Facts:Per Serving: Calories 171, total Carbs 12g, net Carbs 9g, Fiber 3g, Protein , Fat 13g, saturated Fat 1g, sugar 9g, sodium 1mg, Cholesterol 0mg

Dreamy Cinnamon Cheesecake

Servings: 2
Cooking Time: 4 Hours
Ingredients:
- 1/3 of a cup of Graham Cracker crumbs
- 1 tbsp of melted Unsalted Butter
- 1/8 of a tsp of Cinnamon
- Sea Salt as needed
- 6oz of Cream Cheese, at room temperature
- ½ a tbsp of All-purpose Flour
- 1 large Egg
- 1 tsp of Pure Almond Extract
- ½ a cup of Sour Cream

Directions:
1. Mix together the cracker crumbs, a pinch of salt, cinnamon and melted butter
2. Use a spring-form baking dish that will fit inside your crockpot on a stand
3. Spread the base mixture over the bottom and up the sides of the baking dish
4. Beat the flour ¼ of a tsp of salt and cream cheese together, then add the extract, egg and sour cream, beat these until smooth
5. Pour the cheesecake into the baking dish
6. Place half an inch of water in your crockpot and insert the stand
7. Place the cheesecake in the center without the sides touching the bowl
8. Place a triple layer of paper kitchen towels over the crockpot and close the lid
9. Cook on high for 2 hours without opening
10. Turn off the heat and keeping the lid closed (so you do not lose any heat), allow the cheesecake to cool for about an hour before taking it out and cooling further to room temperature
11. Place the cheesecake wrapped in plastic, in the refrigerator (it will absorb smells if not wrapped) for about 4 hours
12. Carefully remove the cheesecake from the baking dish, then serve with your favorite toppings

Nutrition Facts:Per Serving: Cal 362, total fat 34.5g, sat fat 21g, chol 154mg, carb 6.5g, fiber 0.2g, protein 7.9

Swiss Fondue With Kirsch

Servings:2
Cooking Time: 2 Hours
Ingredients:
- 2 cloves of Garlic, sliced in half
- 1 cup of Dry White Wine (nice drinking wine)
- 1 tbsp of fresh Lemon Juice
- 8oz of Swiss Cheese
- 4oz of Cheddar Cheese
- 1 tbsp of Flour
- 2 to 3 tbsp of Kirsch
- A pinch of Nutmeg
- ¼ of a tsp of Black Pepper
- ¼ of a tsp of Paprika
- A loaf of French or Crusty Bread, cubed

Directions:
1. Bring the wine to boil with the garlic in a clean stainless saucepan and add the lemon and simmer gently
2. Combine the cheese and flour in a bowl and slowly add this to the simmering wine stirring constantly
3. Once it is well blended and melted, place it in your crock pot and add the Kirsch, paprika, nutmeg and pepper
4. Cook, covered, on high for 2 hours, then serve in the crock pot with forks and bread cubes

Nutrition Facts:Per Serving: Cal 9, total fat55.3, sat fat 33.4, chol 167mg, sodium 678mg, carb 24.6g, fiber 0.2gg, protein 47g

Glazed Tropical Cookie Bars

Servings: 25
Cooking Time: 4 Hours
Ingredients:
- nonstick cooking spray
- 1 ½ + 1/3 cup flour
- ¾ cup splenda, divided
- 1/8 tsp salt
- ¾ cup butter, cubed
- 2 eggs
- ½ cup low-fat sour cream
- 20 oz. can crushed pineapple, drained well
- ½ cup stevia confectioners' sugar
- 1 tbsp. skim milk
- ½ tsp coconut extract

Directions:
1. spray the crock pot with cooking spray.
2. In a large bowl, combine 1 ½ cups flour, ¼ cup splenda, salt, and butter until mixture resembles coarse crumbs. Reserve 1 cup of the mixture. Press remaining mixture in an even layer on the bottom of the crock pot.
3. In a separate large bowl, whisk together eggs, sour cream, remaining flour, and splenda until well combined.
4. stir in pineapples and spread over crust in the crock pot.
5. sprinkle the reserved crumb mixture over the top of the filling. Place two paper towels over the top and add the lid.
6. Cook on low heat 4 hours, or on high 2 hours, until filling is set and the edges start to brown.
7. Let cool before slicing and transferring to a wire rack.
8. In a small bowl, whisk together the stevia powdered sugar, milk, and coconut extract until smooth. drizzle over bars.

Nutrition Facts:Per Serving: Calories 11 total Carbs 13g, net Carbs 12g, Fiber 1g, Protein 2g, Fat 7g, saturated Fat 2g, sugar 6g, sodium 72mg, Cholesterol 16mg

Key Lime Dump Cake

Servings:4
Cooking Time: 2 Hours
Ingredients:
- 44 oz Key lime filling
- 15 ¼ oz Betty Crocker Vanilla Cake mix
- Cooking spray
- 8 tbsp butter, melted

Directions:
1. Spray the crockpot with cooking spray then spread the lime filling at the bottom.
2. Combine the cake mix and butter in a mixing bowl.
3. Pour the mixture over lime filling and spread it evenly.
4. Cover the crockpot with the lid and set time for two hours.
5. When time elapses, serve and enjoy with whip cream.

Nutrition Facts:Per Serving: Calories 197, Total Fat 23g, Saturated Fat 4g, Total Carbs 18g, Net Carbs 1, Protein 3.4g, Sugar 23g, Fiber 0.3g, Sodium 296mg, Potassium 63mg

No Peel Crockpot Hard-boiled Eggs

Servings:8
Cooking Time: 1 Hour 30 Minutes
Ingredients:
- 8 eggs
- Unsalted butter

Directions:
1. Add two cups of water in your crockpot.
2. Butter an oven-safe bowl that fits your crockpot. Break the eggs to the buttered bowl ensuring the yolks don't break.
3. Cover and cook for an hour and a half or until the eggs look hard-boiled.
4. Loosen the edges with a spatula then remove the safe bowl from the crockpot.
5. Turn the bowl on a cutting board and chop the eggs to your desired consistency.
6. Serve and enjoy the eggs with a salad of choice.

Nutrition Facts:Per Serving: Calories 63, Total Fat 4g, Saturated Fat 1g, Total Carbs 1g, Net Carbs 0g, Protein 6g, Sugar 1g, Fiber 0.1g, Sodium 62 mg, Potassium 61 mg

Black Bean Dip

Servings: 14
Cooking Time: 8 Hours
Ingredients:
- 2 cups dried black beans, soaked overnight
- 2 tbsp. cooking liquid
- Juice from half a lime
- ¼ tsp garlic powder
- ¼ tsp cumin
- ¼ tsp salt

Directions:
1. drain and rinse the beans and add them to the crock pot. Add just enough water to cover the beans.
2. Add the lid and cook on high 8 hours or until beans are tender.
3. drain the beans reserving 2 tablespoons of the cooking liquid.
4. Add the beans, liquid, lime juice, seasonings to a food processor and pulse until smooth.

Nutrition Facts:Per Serving: Calories 122, total Carbs 22g, net Carbs 17g, Fiber , Protein 8g, Fat 1g, saturated Fat 0g, sugar 1g, sodium 52mg, Cholesterol 0mg

Beautiful Apple And Blackberry Crumble

Servings: 2
Cooking Time: 4 Hours
Ingredients:

- 2 Medium Apples, sweet or tart, peeled if you wish and sliced
- ¼ of a cup of Fresh or Frozen Blackberries
- 1/4 of a cup of Old Fashioned Oats
- 1/4 of a cup of Quinoa Flakes
- 1/4 of a cup of mixed Ground Nuts
- 1 tsp of ground Cinnamon
- ½ a tsp of ground Nutmeg
- 1/4 of a cup of Unsalted Butter
- 1/4 of a cup of Powered Erythritol

Directions:

1. Arrange the sliced apples and Blackberries evenly in the bottom of your slow cooker
2. Place the oats, quinoa, ground nuts and seasonings in a bowl and combine well
3. Cut in the butter into the flour mix to produce a crumbly mixture
4. Pour the crumble mixture over the apples
5. Place three paper towels on your crockpot and close the lid, the paper towels will absorb the condensation, keeping the crumble dry
6. Cook on low for 4 hours, then serve in bowls with your favorite topping

Nutrition Facts:Per Serving: Cal 206, total fat 2.2g, sat fat 0.8g, chol 3mg, sodium 3mg, carb 45, fiber 8.2g, protein 3.6g

Peppermint Chocolate Pudding Cake

Servings:4
Cooking Time: 3 Hours
Ingredients:

- 15 ¼ Chocolate cake mix
- ¼ tbsp peppermint extract
- 3 cups milk, low fat
- 3 ½ oz chocolate cook and serve pudding and pie filling mix, sugar-free and fat-free
- 1 cup water
- ⅓ Cup canola oil
- 3 eggs, refrigerated and light beaten

Directions:

1. Coat your crockpot liner with cooking spray and set aside.
2. In a mixing bowl, combine cake mix, peppermint extract, water, oil, and eggs. Pour the mixture in the prepared crockpot.
3. In another bowl, whisk together milk and pudding. Pour in a saucepan and heat until it just simmers. Remove from heat.
4. Pour the pudding mixture over the cake mix mixture. Lid the crockpot and set time for three hours.
5. Remove the liner from the crockpot and let the cake rest to cool. Serve and enjoy.

Nutrition Facts:Per Serving: Calories 185, Total Fat 7g, Saturated Fat 2g, Total Carbs 27g, Net Carbs 22g, Protein 4g, Sugar 14g, Fiber 1g, Sodium 233mg, Potassium 181mg

Delicious Baked Apples

Servings: 2
Cooking Time: 2 Hours
Ingredients:
- 4 small-size Gala Apples
- 1 cup of Granola, can be toasted or raw
- 1 tbsp of melted Unsalted Butter
- 2 tsp of Pomegranate Molasses

Directions:
1. Slice a thin layer off the top of each apple
2. Use a melon baller to remove the core and seeds from the apples
3. Fill the centers of the apples with granola and place them in your crockpot
4. Drizzle a little melted butter and a teaspoon of pomegranate molasses on the granola
5. Cook, covered, for 2 to 2½ hours, until the apple is tender. Don't over cook

Nutrition Facts:Per Serving: Cal 404, total fat .6g, chol 12mg, sodium 64mg, carb 150.8g, fiber 24g

Forbidden Chocolate Lava Cake

Servings: 2
Cooking Time: 3 Hours
Ingredients:
- 1/4 cup of Flour
- 1/2 tsp of Baking Powder
- 2 tbsp of Dutch Bakers Chocolate
- 2 tbsp of Unsalted Butter
- 1oz of Semisweet Dutch Chocolate
- 1/3 of a cup of Powered Erythritol
- 2 tbsp of Dutch Cocoa Powder
- 1 tsp of Pure Vanilla Extract
- 1/8 tsp of Sea Salt
- 1/4 of a cup of Milk
- 1 Egg Yolk
- 1/4 cup Dutch-processed cocoa powder
- 1/4 Powered Erythritol
- 1/8 of a cup Brown Sugar
- 3/4 of a cup of hot water, add more if needed

Directions:
1. Place a liner inside your crockpot or spray the inside with non-stick spray
2. Mix together the flour and baking powder in a bowl
3. Melt together the butter and chocolate together on low power in a microwave
4. Whisk 1/3 of a cup of powered erythritol, 2 tbsp of cocoa powder, the milk, egg yolk, vanilla into the chocolate butter mixture
5. Then add the flour mixture
6. Pour the batter into your lined crockpot and smooth the surface
7. Whisk together the cocoa powder, powered erythritol, brown sugar and hot water until completely combined. Carefully pour the mixture onto the center of the batter in your slow cooker, but do not mix them
8. Cover your crockpot with 3 layers of paper towels and
9. Cook, covered, for 2-3 hours on HIGH, check the progress after 2 hours. When done the cake will come away from the sides of your crockpot bowl
10. Remove the lid carefully and allow it to cool for 30 minutes
11. Serve the cake topped with ice cream or whipped cream

Nutrition Facts:Per Serving: Cal 335, total fat 17.7g, sat fat 10.7g, chol 140mg, sodium 223mg, carb 39g, fiber 0.08g, protein 4.9gg

Chocolate Coconut Cake

Servings: 12
Cooking Time: 5 Hours
Ingredients:

- 1 ¾ cup oats
- 3 tbsp. coconut oil, melted
- ½ cup applesauce, unsweetened
- ½ cup cocoa powder, unsweetened
- ½ cup stevia
- 1 tbsp. vanilla
- ½ cup plain Greek yogurt
- ½ tsp cream of tartar
- 1 ½ tsp baking powder
- 1 ½ tsp baking soda
- ½ tsp salt
- 1 cup hot water
- ½ cup chocolate chips, sugar-free
- ¼ cup coconut flakes, unsweetened

Directions:

1. Line the crock pot with parchment paper.
2. Place all of the ingredients, except the chocolate chips and coconut, in a food processor or blender. Pulse until well combined and the oats are completely ground.
3. stir in the chocolate chips and pour evenly into the crock pot. sprinkle the coconut over the top.
4. Add the lid and cook on low heat 5 hours, or on high 2-3 hours, until the cake passes the toothpick test.
5. Let cool at least 1minutes, then using the parchment paper, lift the cake from the pot and place on a wire rack to cool completely.

Nutrition Facts:Per Serving: Calories 199, total Carbs 2, net Carbs 21g, Fiber 5g, Protein 6g, Fat 10g, saturated Fat 6g, sugar 5g, sodium 224mg, Cholesterol 1mg

Autumn Baked Apples

Servings: 6
Cooking Time: 5 Hours
Ingredients:

- 6 Granny smith apples, cored
- ½ cup cranberries, dried
- ½ cup walnuts, coarsely chopped
- 2 tbsp. stevia brown sugar
- 1 tbsp. orange zest
- 1 cup water

Directions:

1. Peel just the top ¼ of each apple.
2. In a small bowl, combine cranberries, walnuts, stevia, and orange zest and mix well.
3. stuff the mixture into the apples and place them in the crock pot.
4. Pour the water around the apples. Add the lid and cook on low heat 5 hours.

Nutrition Facts:Per Serving: Calories 186, total Carbs 27g, net Carbs 21g, Fiber 6g, Protein 2g, Fat 7g, saturated Fat 1g, sugar 26g, sodium g, Cholesterol 0mg

Easy Spicy Refried Tex-mex Bean Dip

Servings: 2
Cooking Time: 1 To 2 Hours
Ingredients:
- ½ a cup of Refried Beans
- 1 tbsp of Taco Seasoning
- 1 small diced Onion
- 1 cup of shredded Monterey Jack Cheese
- Tabasco Sauce to Taste
- 1 Jalapeno or Mild Chile diced or more to taste

Directions:
1. Place everything in your crockpot and stir to combine
2. Cook, covered, on low about an hour until the cheese is melted, then stir until smooth and serve from your crockpot on low

Nutrition Facts:Per Serving: Cal 245, total fat 6g, sat fat , unsat 2g, chol 15mg, sodium 108mg, carb 34g. fiber10g, protein 16g

Eggplant & Spinach Dip

Servings: 8
Cooking Time: 3 Hours
Ingredients:
- 1 eggplant, peeled and cubed
- 1 tbsp. olive oil, divided
- ¼ tsp salt
- 2 cups baby spinach
- 3 cloves garlic, diced fine
- 1/3 cup fat-free parmesan cheese, grated
- nonstick cooking spray

Directions:
1. Heat oven to 400°F. Line a baking sheet with foil.
2. In a large bowl, add the eggplant, ½ tablespoon oil, and salt and toss to coat. spread in an even layer on the baking sheet and cook 10-15 minutes or until the eggplant starts to brown.
3. Heat the remaining oil in a large skillet over medium heat. Add the spinach and garlic and cook until spinach is wilted about minutes.
4. Place the roasted eggplant in a food processor and pulse until smooth. If the mixture is too thick, add a tablespoon of water, one at a time, until the mixture is smooth and creamy.
5. Add the spinach and half the parmesan to the eggplant and pulse just until combined.
6. spray the crock pot with cooking spray.
7. transfer the eggplant mixture to the crock pot, add the lid, and cook on how to heat 3 hours, or until hot and bubbly.
8. sprinkle the remaining parmesan over the top and serve.

Nutrition Facts:Per Serving: Calories 58, total Carbs 6g, net Carbs3 g, Fiber 3g, Protein 3g, Fat 3g, saturated Fat 1g, sugar 3g, sodium 131mg, Cholesterol 3mg

Seafood Supreme Dip

Servings: 2
Cooking Time: 2 Hours
Ingredients:
- ¼ of a cup of cream of Shrimp Soup
- ¼ of a cup of grated Tasty Cheddar Cheese
- ¼ of a cup of grated American Cheese
- ¼ of a cup of cooked diced Lobster
- ¼ of a cup of chopped cooked Shrimp or Crab Meat
- A dash of Paprika
- A dash of Nutmeg
- A dash of Cayenne Pepper
- A loaf of French or Crusty Bread, cubed for dipping

Directions:
1. Place everything except the cubed bread in your crockpot and cook, covered, on high for 2 hours, stirring occasionally

Nutrition Facts:Per Serving: Cal 115, total fat 3.5g, sat fat 1.4g, unsat 1g, chol 34mg, carb 17, sodium 427mg, protein 7.7g

Chipotle Bbq Pork Folded Tacos

Servings:4
Cooking Time: 4 Hours
Ingredients:
- 2 garlic cloves
- 1 cup barbecue sauce, reduced sugar
- 4 chipotle chili peppers, purred
- 2 lb. pork shoulder, trimmed
- 16 whole-wheat tortillas, low carb
- 1 ½ tbsp smoked paprika
- 1 ½ cup onions, diced
- 2 cups cabbage, shredded

Directions:
1. Combine garlic cloves, sauce, and chipotle peppers in a blender and blend well. Let rest in a refrigerator.
2. Place the pork in your crockpot and cook on high for four hours. Transfer the pork on your cutting board.
3. Use a fork to shred the pork discarding excess fat. Return the pot to your crockpot.
4. Sprinkle the smoked paprika and barbecue sauce mixture then cook on low for one hour. Skim off excess fat.
5. Warm the tortillas and place a heaping spoonful of cooked pork. Top with onions and cabbage.
6. Serve and enjoy.

Nutrition Facts:Per Serving: Calories 160, Total Fat , Saturated Fat 2g, Total Carbs 15g, Net Carbs 7g, Protein 15g, Sugar 3g, Fiber 8g, Sodium 350mg, Potassium 230 mg

Raspberry Oat Snack Bars

Servings: 16
Cooking Time: 4 Hours
Ingredients:
- nonstick cooking spray
- 1 cup white whole wheat flour
- 1 cup oats
- ½ cup stevia
- ½ tsp baking powder
- ¼ tsp salt
- ½ cup coconut oil, melted
- 2/3 cup raspberry jam, sugar-free

Directions:
1. spray the crock pot with cooking spray.
2. In a large bowl, whisk together flour, oats, stevia, baking powder, and salt.
3. stir in the coconut oil. Press half the mixture on the bottom of the crock pot.
4. Carefully spread the jam over the bottom crust and sprinkle remaining oat mixture evenly over the top, press lightly.
5. Add the lid and cook on low heat 4 hours or until the bars are set and starting to brown around the edges.
6. Let cool 15 minutes before slicing and transferring to a wire rack to cool completely.

Nutrition Facts:Per Serving: Calories 212, total Carbs 20g, net Carbs 18g, Fiber 2g, Protein 2g, Fat 14g, saturated Fat 12g, sugar 6g, sodium 59mg, Cholesterol 0mg

Heavenly Poached Pears

Servings: 2
Cooking Time: 3 Hours
Ingredients:
- 4 small Pears, skinned but with the stem
- ½ a cup of fresh Apple Juice
- 1 Stick of Cinnamon
- 2 tbsp of chopped Walnuts

Directions:
1. Slice a small section from the base of each pear so it will stand on its end
2. Place the apple juice in your crockpot with the cinnamon stick and lay each pear on its side in the juice
3. Cook, covered, for 1 hour on low, then turn the pears over and cook, covered for another hour or until tender
4. When cooked, place the pears on plates
5. Pass the liquid through a sieve into a saucepan
6. Simmer the sauce with the cinnamon stick and walnuts until it's reduced to a nice consistency
7. Pour the sauce over the pears and serve

Nutrition Facts:Per Serving: 236 cal, 6.9g total fat, 0.6g sat fat, 4mg sodium, 33g carb, 8.5g fiber, 4.6 protein

Fudge Cake

Servings:8
Cooking Time: 1hour 30 Minutes
Ingredients:
- 15 ¼ oz Betty Crocker Chocolate Fudge Cake
- 4 oz Jell-O Chocolate Instant pudding mix
- ⅔ Cup sour cream
- 11 ½ oz Smuckers Hot Fudge Sauce
- 4 eggs
- ¾ Cup Vegetable Oil

Directions:
1. Combine all ingredients in a mixing bowl and let sit for two minutes.
2. Spray your crockpot with cooking spray then transfer the mixture to the crockpot.
3. Cover the crockpot and set the timer for one and a half hours. When time elapses, transfer the cake to serving bowls and drizzle with hot fudge sauce.

Nutrition Facts:Per Serving: Calories 150, Total Fat 1g, Saturated Fat 2.2g, Total Carbs 26.9g, Net Carbs 22.1g, Protein 5.4g, Sugar 14g, Fiber 3.3g, Sodium 154mg, Potassium 0mg

Butterscotch Almond Brownies

Servings: 24
Cooking Time: 3 Hours
Ingredients:
- nonstick cooking spray
- 1 cup butter, soft
- 3 cups splenda brown sugar blend
- 4 eggs
- 3 tbsp. vanilla
- 1 ½ cups flour
- 3 teaspoons baking powder
- 1 ½ cups almonds, chopped

Directions:
1. spray crock pot with cooking spray.
2. In a large bowl, beat butter and splenda until creamy.
3. Add eggs and vanilla and mix to combine.
4. stir in remaining ingredients until combined.
5. spread the batter evenly in the pot. Add the lid and cook on low 2-3 hours until brownies pass the toothpick test. Let cool completely before slicing.

Nutrition Facts:Per Serving: Calories 182, total Carbs 14g, net Carbs 10g, Fiber 4g, Protein , Fat 12g, saturated Fat 2g, sugar 1g, sodium 138mg, Cholesterol 0mg

Pumpkin Streusel Bars

Servings: 16
Cooking Time: 4 Hours
Ingredients:

- nonstick cooking spray
- 1 1/3 cups white whole wheat flour, divided
- 1 tsp baking powder
- ½ tsp baking soda
- 1 tsp cinnamon, divided
- 1/8 tsp ginger
- ¼ tsp salt
- 1 cup stevia, divided
- 2 eggs
- ½ cup coconut oil, melted
- ½ can pumpkin puree
- ½ teaspoon vanilla
- 4 tbsp. butter, unsalted

Directions:

1. spray the crock pot with cooking spray.
2. In a medium bowl, whisk together 1 cup flour, baking powder, baking soda, ½ teaspoon cinnamon, ginger, and salt until combined.
3. In a large bowl, beat together the eggs, stevia, oil, pumpkin, and vanilla until light and frothy.
4. Add the dry ingredients and continue mixing until combined. Pour batter evenly in the crock pot.
5. In a small bowl, use a fork to mix the remaining 1/3 cup flour, ¼ cup stevia, ½ teaspoon cinnamon, and butter until combined. sprinkle evenly over the top of the batter.
6. Add the lid and cook on low heat 3-4 hours, or on high 2-3 hours or until the bars pass the toothpick test.
7. Let cool 15 minutes before slicing and serving.

Nutrition Facts:Per Serving: Calories 150, total Carbs 19g, net Carbs 1, Fiber 1g, Protein 2g, Fat 8g, saturated Fat 2g, sugar 2g, sodium 83mg, Cholesterol 22mg

Easy Homemade Applesauce

Servings: 10
Cooking Time: 8 Hours
Ingredients:

- 6 Granny smith apples, peel & core
- 6 Gala apples, peel & core
- 1 tbsp. water
- 1 tsp cinnamon
- 1/8 tsp nutmeg

Directions:

1. Place all the ingredients in the crock pot and stir to mix well.
2. Add the lid and cook on low heat 6-8 hours or until the apples are tender. serve warm or cold.

Nutrition Facts:Per Serving: Calories 89, total Carbs 2, net Carbs 19g, Fiber 4g, Protein 0g, Fat 0g, saturated Fat 0g, sugar 17g, sodium 2mg, Cholesterol 0mg

Alluring Baked Oatmeal Bars

Servings: 2
Cooking Time: 8 Hours
Ingredients:
- 1 Egg
- ¼ of a tsp of Vanilla Extract
- 1 small Mashed Banana
- 1 cup of Milk
- 1 cup of Rolled Oats
- ¼ of a cup of Flaxseeds
- 1 tsp of ground Cinnamon
- ½ a tsp of Baking Powder
- ½ a tsp of Sea Salt

Directions:
1. Place a piece of parchment paper inside your crockpot so it covers the botomand goes up the side a little
2. Place all the ingredients except the optional topping in a bowl and mix them together
3. Pour the mixed batter onto the parchment paper in your crockpot
4. Place your chosen topping in the batter (you can place different things in different areas for variety)
5. Cook, covered, on low for 8 hours
6. Remove from your crockpot using the edges of the parchment paper as handles and cut it into bars on chopping board

Nutrition Facts:Per Serving: Cal 168, total fat 4.6g, sat fat 0.6g, chol 2mg, carb25.1g, fiber 5g, protein 9g

Broccoli Cheese Dip

Servings: 10
Cooking Time: 3 Hours
Ingredients:
- 1 tsp extra virgin olive oil
- 1 onion, diced fine
- 6 cups broccoli florets
- 10 ½ oz. can condensed broccoli cheese soup
- 1 cup cheddar cheese, grated
- ½ cup skim milk
- ½ cup sour cream
- 1 tbsp. Worcestershire sauce
- 1 tsp garlic powder
- 1 tsp basil

Directions:
1. Heat the oil in a large skillet over med-high heat.
2. Add the onion and cook until translucent, about 5 minutes.
3. Add the broccoli and cook, occasionally stirring, another 5 minutes. Remove from heat.
4. Add the remaining ingredients to the crock pot and stir to combine. Add the broccoli and onions and stir well.
5. Add the lid and cook on low heat 2-3 hours until cheese is melted and broccoli is tender. stir well before serving.

Nutrition Facts:Per Serving: Calories 124, total Carbs 8g, net Carbs 7g, Fiber 1g, Protein , Fat 8g, saturated Fat 4g, sugar 2g, sodium 326mg, Cholesterol 20mg

Italian Turkey Meatballs

Servings: 4
Cooking Time: 4 Hours
Ingredients:
- nonstick cooking spray
- 1 lb. ground turkey
- ¼ cup onion, diced fine
- 2 cloves garlic, diced fine
- ½ cup whole wheat panko bread crumbs, pulsed lightly in a food processor
- 2 egg whites
- ½ tsp salt
- ¼ tsp black pepper
- ¼ tsp crushed red pepper flakes
- 2 tsp Italian seasoning
- 24 oz. marinara sauce, sugar-free
- ½ cup chicken broth, low sodium
- ½ cup parmesan cheese, reduced fat

Directions:
1. set oven to broil and spray a baking sheet with cooking spray
2. In a large bowl, combine turkey, onion, garlic, bread crumbs, egg whites, salt, pepper, red pepper flakes, and Italian seasoning.
3. Form mixture into 1-inch balls and place on the prepared baking sheet. Broil 5 minutes or until lightly brown on the outside.
4. transfer the meatballs to the crock pot and add the marinara sauce and broth. stir gently to mix.
5. Add the lid and cook on low heat 4 hours. sprinkle with parmesan and serve.

Nutrition Facts:Per Serving: Calories 284, total Carbs 11g, net Carbs 10g, Fiber 1g, Protein 31g, Fat 13g, saturated Fat 5g, sugar 4g, sodium 448mg, Cholesterol 89mg

Chocolate Quinoa Brownies

Servings:2
Cooking Time: 4 Hours
Ingredients:
- 1 cup of cooked Quinoa
- 1 small Egg
- ½ a tsp of Vanilla Extract
- ¾ of a cup of Sugar Free Chocolate Chips
- 2 tbsp of Unsweetened Cocoa Powder
- A large pinch of Sea Salt
- 1/8 of a tsp of Baking Powder
- 1/8 of a cup of ground Flaxseed
- ¼ of a cup of Unsweetened Apple Sauce
- 1/4 of a cup of Heavy Cream
- 1/4 of a cup of Unsweetened Cocoa Powder
- 1 tsp of Liquid Chocolate Stevia
- ½ a tsp of Vanilla Extract

Directions:
1. Process all the ingredients together in your food processor and allow it to rest while you line your crockpot bottom with parchment paper
2. Pour and spread the mixture on the parchment paper and smooth over the surface
3. Cook, covered, for 2 hours on high or 4 hours on low
4. Cool on a wire rack, then frost and slice into portions
5. Frosting
6. Combine all the ingredients and melt over a lot heat or in your microwave

Nutrition Facts:Per Serving: Cal 149, total fat 4.2g, sat fat 0.8g, sodium 19mg, Carb 22.1g
7. Fiber 2.9g, protein 5.6g

Creme Brulee

Servings:4
Cooking Time: 2 Hours
Ingredients:
- 4 egg yolks
- ¼ cup white sugar
- 1 ⅔ cups whipping cream, heavy
- 2 tbsp vanilla extract
- ¼ tbsp salt

Directions:
1. In a mixing bowl, whisk together egg yolks, quarter cup sugar, and salt.
2. Whisk in whipping cream and vanilla extract. Strain the custard mixture into a measuring cup.
3. Line the crockpot bottom with folded kitchen towel. Place the ramekins on the towel and fill the crockpot with water such that the water comes halfway the ramekins.
4. Pour the custard mixture into ramekins then drape the towel over the crockpot. Place the lid the crockpot.
5. Set the timer for two hours so that the custard jiggles a little bit but is set.
6. Remove the ramekins from the crockpot and let them rest to completely cool.

Nutrition Facts:Per Serving: Calories 255, Total Fat 41.1g, Saturated Fat 24g, Total Carbs 20g, Net Carbs 0g, Protein 4., Sugar 4g, Fiber 0g, Sodium 191mg, Potassium 96mg

Maple Custard

Servings:6
Cooking Time: 2 Hours
Ingredients:
- 1 cup heavy cream, organic
- ½ cup whole milk, organic
- ¼ cup sukrin Gold
- ½ tbsp cinnamon
- 2 egg yolks
- 2 eggs
- 1 tbsp maple extract
- 1 tbsp salt

Directions:
1. Combine all ingredients in a blender and blend until well combined.
2. Grease ramekins with butter then pour the mixture into each ramekin up to three-quarters full.
3. Place four ramekins at the bottom of the crockpot and the remaining two on top of the bottom ramekins but against the crockpot sides.
4. Place the lid and set the timer for two hours on high. When time elapses, remove the ramekins from the crockpot.
5. Let rest for one hour to cool. Sprinkle more cinnamon then serve and enjoy.

Nutrition Facts:Per Serving: Calories 190, Total Fat 18g, Saturated Fat 10g, Total Carbs 2g, Net Carbs 0g, Protein 4g, Sugar 1g, Fiber 0g, Sodium 144mg, Potassium 83mg

Peanut Butter Chocolate Cake

Servings: 16
Cooking Time: 4 Hours
Ingredients:
- nonstick cooking spray
- 1 cup whole wheat pastry flour
- ½ cup cocoa powder, unsweetened
- 1 tbsp. baking powder
- ½ cup honey
- 2 egg whites
- 1/3 cup peanut butter, sugar-free
- 2 tsp vanilla
- ¾ cup apple sauce, unsweetened

Directions:
1. Line the bottom of the crock pot with parchment paper and spray with cooking spray.
2. In a large bowl, whisk together flour, cocoa powder, and baking powder until combined.
3. In a separate bowl, whisk together honey, egg whites, peanut butter, vanilla, and applesauce.
4. stir the dry ingredients into the honey mixture until well combined.
5. Pour the batter into the crock pot and add the lid. Cook on low heat 4 hours, or until the cake passes the toothpick test.
6. Let cool 15 minutes in the pot before transferring to a wire rack to cool completely.

Nutrition Facts:Per Serving: Calories 141, total Carbs 19g, net Carbs 16g, Fiber 3g, Protein 3g, Fat 3g, saturated Fat 2g, sugar 10g, sodium 0mg, Cholesterol 0mg

Cardamom Apple Bread Pudding

Servings: 6
Cooking Time: 4 Hours
Ingredients:
- Butter flavored cooking spray
- 6 slices whole-wheat bread, cut in 1-inch cubes
- 1 ½ cups coconut milk, reduced fat
- 3 eggs, lightly beaten
- 1 cup applesauce, unsweetened
- ¾ tsp cardamom
- 1 tsp cinnamon
- ¼ tsp nutmeg
- 1 cup apples, peel, core & chop

Directions:
1. spray the crock pot with cooking spray.
2. Place the bread, in an even layer, in the pot.
3. In a large bowl, whisk together milk, eggs, applesauce, and spices until well combined.
4. Fold in the apples and pour the mixture evenly over the bread, pressing gently to make sure all of the bread is covered.
5. Add the lid and cook on low heat 4-hours, or on high 2-3 hours or until the pudding passes the toothpick test. Let cool at least 15 minutes before serving.

Nutrition Facts:Per Serving: Calories 25 total Carbs 23g, net Carbs 20g, Fiber 3g, Protein 8g, Fat 16g, saturated Fat 12g, sugar 7g, sodium 190mg, Cholesterol 93mg

Spicy Pecan Halves

Servings: 2
Cooking Time: 2.5 Hours
Ingredients:
- 1 cup of Pecan Halves
- 2 tbsp of Unsalted Butter
- ½ a tsp of Sea Salt
- 11/2 a tsp of Dried Basil
- ½ a tsp of Dried Oregano
- ½ a tsp of Dried Thyme
- ½ a tsp of Onion Powder
- ¼ of a tsp of Cayenne Pepper, more or less to taste

Directions:
1. Place all the ingredients in your crockpot and mix thoroughly
2. Cook, covered, on high for 15 minutes, then turn to low and cook for hours
3. Cool and serve

Nutrition Facts:Per Serving: Cal 600, total fat62g, sat fat 9g, unsat fat 33g, chol 20mg, sodiummgCarb13g, fiber 8g Protein 7g

Soups & Stews

Dreamy Mediterranean Fish Soup

Servings:2
Cooking Time: 4.5 Hours
Ingredients:
- ¼lb of Cod fillets, cubed
- ¼lb of Shrimp
- 1 small diced Onion
- 1 small Green diced Capsicum
- 2 cloves of minced Garlic
- ½ of a cup of Diced Tomatoes
- 1 cup of Chicken Stock or Broth
- ¼ of a cup of Tomato Sauce
- ¼ of a cup of canned Mushrooms
- 1 tbsp of a cup of sliced Black Olives
- ¼ of a cup of fresh Orange Juice
- ¼ of a cup of Dry White Wine (nice drinking wine)
- 1 Bay Leaf
- 1 tsp of Dried Basil
- 1/8 of a tsp of Fennel Seed, crushed
- 1/8 of a tsp of Freshly Cracked Black Pepper

Directions:
1. Place everything except the fish and shrimp in your crockpot and cook for about 4 to 4.2 hours
2. Add the fresh fish 45 minutes before serving and the fresh shrimp 15 minutes before serving
3. Remove the bay leaf and serve

Nutrition Facts:Per Serving:207cal, 3.1g total fat, 0.6 sat fat, 128.1mg chol, 1200.2mg sodium, 12.2 carb, 2.5g fiber, 28.9g protein

Fantastic Chicken Orzo Soup

Servings: 2
Cooking Time: 4.5 Hours
Ingredients:
- ¼lb of Chicken breasts, trimmed
- 2 cups of low-sodium Chicken Stock or Broth
- 1 Ripe chopped Tomatoes
- 1 Onion, halved and sliced
- The juice and Zest of 1 Lemon
- 1 tsp of Herbes de Provence or mixed Italian Herbs
- ½ a tsp of Sea Salt
- ½ a tsp of freshly cracked Black Pepper
- ¾ of a cup of Whole-Wheat Orzo
- ⅓ of a cup of Black or Green Olives stoned and quartered
- 1 tbsp of chopped fresh Parsley for garnish

Directions:
1. Slice the chicken into ch cubes
2. Place the chicken, tomatoes, onion, stock, lemon juice and zest, herbs de Provence, sea salt and black pepper in your crockpot
3. Cook covered on high for 2 hours or low for 4 hours
4. Then stir in the olives and orzo and allow it to cook a further 30 minutes
5. Allow the soup cool slightly and serve it garnished with the parsley

Nutrition Facts:Per Serving:278 cal, 5g fat, 1g sat fat. 7g fiber, 29g carb, 29g protein, mg chol, 434 sodium, 29g protein

Romantic Greek Lemon Chicken Soup

Servings:2
Cooking Time: 3 Hours
Ingredients:

- ½lb of skinless Chicken Breasts
- 1 small chopped Yellow Onion
- 1 small chopped stick of Celery leaves included
- 1 clove of minced Garlic
- 1 cup of Low Sodium, Chicken Stock or Broth
- 1 cups of Water
- 2 tbsp of fresh Lemon Juice
- 1 Egg
- Sea Salt and Cracked Black Pepper to taste

Directions:

1. Place the chicken, celery, onion, garlic, stock and water in your crockpot and season it with tsp of salt and ¼ of a tsp of pepper
2. Cook the chicken about 3 hours on high or 4 to 5 hours on low
3. When the chicken is cooked through and tender, take it from the cooker and allow it cool slightly
4. Slice the chicken into chunks and return it to the crockpot
5. Whisk the eggs lightly in a bowl with the lemon juice before temper them by adding several drops of hot soup at a time while constantly beating the eggs. Keep beating the eggs while adding a little hot soup until you have added about a cupful, then mix the eggs into the soup in your crockpot
6. Taste and if necessary adjust the seasoning, then serve

Nutrition Facts:Per Serving:16cal, 4g Total fat, 1g Sat fat, 99mgcho, 229 Sodium, 14g carb, 1g fiber, 20g protein

Hearty Vegetarian Minestrone

Servings:2
Cooking Time: 7 Hours
Ingredients:

- 1 cup of Vegetable Stock or Broth
- ¼ of a cup of Soaked White Dried Beans
- ¼ of a cup of Soaked Red Dried Beans
- 3 medium, ripe, quartered Tomatoes
- 1 chunky diced Onion
- 1 large chopped stick of Celery Leaves included
- 1 diced Carrot
- ½ a cup of chopped Green Beans
- ½ a cup of chopped Baby Spinach
- 1 diced Zucchini
- 3 finely diced cloves of Garlic
- 1 tbsp of chopped Parsley
- 1 tsp of Oregano
- 1 sprigs of Thyme
- Sea salt and freshly cracked Black Pepper to taste
- Freshly shaved Parmesan Cheese for topping when serving

Directions:

1. Combine everything except the spinach leaves in your crockpot, put on the lid and cook the soup for 4 to 5 hours on high or 7 to 8 hours on low
2. Stir the baby spinach into the minestrone and cook about another 15 minutes
3. Sprinkle the herbs and Parmesan over and serve

Nutrition Facts:Per Serving:219 cal, 8.9g total fat, 3.1 sat fat, mg chol, 33mg sodium, 31.6 carb. 4.2 fiber, 5.1g protein

Pork And Green Chile Stew

Servings:6
Cooking Time: 4 Hours 25 Minutes
Ingredients:

- 2 pounds boneless sirloin pork roast or shoulder roast
- 15 ounces can hominy or whole -kernel corn drained
- 2tbsp quick-cooking tapioca
- 8 ounce diced green chile peppers
- ¼ tbsp dried oregano, crushed
- 1tbsp vegetable oil
- ½ cup chopped onion, medium size
- 4cups peeled and cubed tomatoes, medium size
- 3 cups water
- 1 tbsp garlic salt
- ½ tbsp ancho chile powder
- ½ tbsp ground cumin and pepper
- ¼ tbsp dried oregano, crushed
- Chopped fresh cilantro, optional

Directions:

1. Remove excess fat from meat and cut into ½ -inch pieces
2. Add oil in large skillet and heat over medium-high heat. Sauté the onions and add half of the meat Cook until browned.
3. Remove the meat from the skillet using a slotted spoon. Repeat the process with the remaining meat.
4. Drain off fat and transfer meat to crockpot.
5. While stirring add in tomatoes, water hominy, tapioca, green chile peppers, garlic salt, ancho chili powder, cumin, ground pepper, and oregano.
6. Cover and cook on high for 4 to 5 hours or low for 7 to 8 hours.
7. Embellish each serving with cilantro.

Nutrition Facts:Per Serving: Calories 1g, total fats 4g, saturated fats 1g, total carbs 23g, net carbs 20g, protein 15g, sugar 2g, fiber; 3g, sodium 251mg, potassium 782mg.

Delectable Chicken, Chorizo And Kale Soup

Servings:2
Cooking Time: 8 Hours
Ingredients:

- 2oz pork Chorizo without the casing (a fermented, cured, smoked sausage)
- 1 cloves of sliced Garlic
- 1 sliced Onion
- 2 cups of Chicken Stock
- 1 Bay Leaf
- 1 tsp of Sweet Paprika
- 1 medium diced Potatoes
- 2oz of thinly sliced Baby Kale
- Sea Salt and Freshly cracked Black Pepper to taste

Directions:

1. Preheat your crockpot on the sauté setting, then add the oil and sauté the onions until golden
2. Add the chorizo and the garlic, stir for about a minute and add the stock, bay leaf and potatoes
3. Cook covered for 4 to 5 hours on high or 7 to 8 hours on low
4. About 30 minutes before serving, adjust the seasoning if necessary, add the kale, give a stir and cook again for about 10 minutes
5. Then remove half of the chorizo and the bay leaf
6. Using your immersion (stick blender) or bench top blender, puree the soup, leaving just a few chunks
7. Place the remaining chorizo to the soup and serve

Nutrition Facts:Per Serving:223 cal, 9.1g total fat, 2. sat fat, 997mg sodium, 24mg chol, 26.9 carb, 4.9g fiber, 9.9g protein

Homely Italian Butternut Soup With Chicken And Salami

Servings: 2
Cooking Time: 8 Hours
Ingredients:
- 1 cup of peeled and cubed Butternut Squash
- 1/2 a cup of Chicken, chopped into 1in pieces
- 1 sticks of diced Celery
- 1 small diced Carrot
- 1 small diced Onion
- 1 clove of finely chopped Garlic
- 2 tsp of Olive Oil
- 1 cup of Chicken Stock
- 1 cup of diced Tomatoes
- A pinch of grated Nutmeg
- ¼ of a tsp of Italian Seasoning
- A pinch of Red Pepper Flakes
- ¼ of a cup of diced Salami
- ¼ of a cup of Milk
- 1 Green Onion, sliced for garnishing

Directions:
1. Sauté the chicken using the oil in a pan or use the sauté option on your crockpot, until browned
2. Take out the chicken and let it cool if sautéed in the crock pot then add the squash, carrots, onions, and celery and sauté these for 3-4 minutes
3. Add the garlic and sauté until fragrant
4. Chop the chicken into cubes or strips and place everything except the salami and milk in your crockpot
5. Cook on high for 4 hours or low for 7 hours
6. Then add the milk and salami, then cook it for a further hour
7. Serve in individual soup bowls with sliced green onions as a garnish.

Nutrition Facts:Per Serving:121 cal, 6.2g total fat, 11mg chol, 402mg sodium, 11.7g carb, 2.4g fiber, 5.5g protein

Delightful Thick Beef And Vegetable Soup

Servings:2
Cooking Time: 8 Hours
Ingredients:
- 1/2lb of diced Beef
- ½ a cup of Fire Roasted Diced Tomatoes
- 1 cup of Beef Stock or Broth
- 1 sliced Carrots
- 1 sliced Celery Stalks
- 1 small diced Onion
- 2 cloves of minced Garlic
- 2 tsp of crushed dried Rosemary
- 1 small bunch of baby Spinach
- Sea Salt to taste and freshly cracked Black Pepper to taste
- 1 tsp of Balsamic Vinegar

Directions:
1. Turn your Sauté option on your crockpot
2. Add the oil and when hot, add the beef
3. Sauté the beef, browning on all sides
4. Add all the other ingredients except the baby spinach and vinegar and stir to mix
5. Cook the soup covered until the beef is tender, on low for 7 to 8 hours
6. Just before serving, stir in the vinegar and baby spinach
7. Allow the soup to stand for 10 minutes, so the spinach warms through and serve

Nutrition Facts:Per Serving:547 cal, 34.6g total fat, 140mg chol, 679mg sodium, 12. carb, 4.3g fiber, 43.7g protein

Home-style Chicken And Mushroom Soup

Servings: 2
Cooking Time: 8 Hours
Ingredients:

- 1 cups of Chicken Stock
- ½ a cup of Water
- 1 small chopped Onion
- 1 clove of minced Garlic
- 1 tsp of Unsalted Butter or clarified Butter
- 2oz of sliced baby Portabella Mushrooms
- 1 cup of shredded Cooked Chicken
- 1 tsp of Dijon mustard
- 1 tbsp of chopped fresh parsley
- Sea Salt and Black Pepper to taste

Directions:

1. Sauté the onion in the butter until tender
2. Add the garlic and cook it for 60 seconds
3. Place everything in your crockpot and stir to combine
4. Cook on low for 6 to 8 hours or high for 3 to hours
5. Add salt and pepper to taste and serve

Nutrition Facts:Per Serving:305 Cal, 8.9g, 3.4g sat fat, 115mg chol, 924mg sodium, 4g carb, 1.4g fiber, 47.9 protein

Beefed-up Vegetable Stew

Servings:6
Cooking Time: 5hours 5 Minutes
Ingredients:

- 1lb lean ground beef
- 16-ounce stew vegetables, frozen
- 14 ounce can diced tomato with garlic, basil, and oregano
- 1 cube beef broth, reduced-sodium
- ½ tbsp garlic powder
- 1 cup of water
- ½ tbsp onion powder
- ¼ tbsp black pepper

Directions:

1. Spray a nonstick skillet with cooking spray over medium heat. Brown the beef and drain it.
2. Spray your crockpot with cooking spray then add beef, stew vegetables, tomatoes, water, beef broth, garlic powder, onion powder, and black pepper.
3. Stir until well combined and cover.
4. Cook on low for five hours.
5. When the time elapses, serve and enjoy.

Nutrition Facts:Per Serving: Calories 199, total fats 8.0g saturated fats 3.1g, total carbs 14g, net carbs 9.8g, protein 18g, sugar 2.2g, sodium 115mg, potassium 7mg.

Comforting, Traditional, Split Pea Soup

Servings: 2
Cooking Time: 8 Hours
Ingredients:
- 1 (8-ounce) pack of Dried Split Peas
- 1 large chopped Carrot
- 1 large chopped Onion
- ½ a cup of chopped Celery
- ½ a cup of Low-Sodium Diced and Cooked Ham
- 2 cups Low Sodium Chicken Broth or Stock
- 1 & 1/2 cups of Fresh Water
- Sea Salt and Black Pepper to taste
- 1 Bay Leaf

Directions:
1. Place all the ingredients in your slow cooker
2. Cook covered on the low setting for 8 hours or until the peas are tender and the soup has thickened
3. Serve

Nutrition Facts:Per Serving: Cal 7, total fat 3.3g, sat fat 1.2g, Chol 25mg, sodium 309mg, carb 71.2g Fiber 27.9g, protein 36.4g

Vegetarian & Vegan Recipes
Magic Whole Stuffed Squash

Servings: 2
Cooking Time: 8 Hours
Ingredients:
- 1 small ripe Winter Squash or Butter Nut Squash that fits whole in your crockpot
- 1 small diced Onion
- 1 small diced Red Capsicum (Pepper)
- 1 small diced Green Capsicum (Pepper)
- 1 small diced Carrot
- 1 stalk of diced Celery
- ½ a cup of diced tomatoes
- 1 bunch of green leafy vegetables, chopped
- ¼ of a cup of pine nuts
- 1/8 tsp of ground ginger
- 1/8 of a tsp of ground cinnamon
- 1/8 tsp of ground Coriander
- 1/8 of a tsp of ground Cumin
- Sea Salt to taste
- Black Pepper to Taste

Directions:
1. Slice the top from the pumpkin to make a lid and scoop out the seeds and stringy bits
2. Place all the ingredients inside the pumpkin and put the top back on, then place it in your crockpot and cook it covered on low for 8 hours or until soft and tender

Nutrition Facts:Per Serving: Cal 2, Total fat1.3g, sat fat 0.2g, Sodium 92mg, Carb 56.5g, Fiber 10.2g, protein 6g

Fabulous Vindaloo Vegetables

Servings:2
Cooking Time: 6 Hours

Ingredients:

- 1 clove of Garlic
- 1 tsp of chopped fresh Ginger,
- 1 pitted Date, coarsely chopped
- 1/2 a tsp of Ground Coriander
- ¼ of a tsp of Ground Cumin
- ¼ of a tsp of Dry Mustard
- A dash of Cayenne Pepper or to taste
- ½ a tsp of Turmeric Powder
- A dash of ground Cardamom
- 1 tbsp of White Wine Vinegar
- 1 small diced Onion
- 1 small, thinly sliced Carrot
- ½ of a cup of Cauliflower Florets
- 1/2 a cup cooked Kidney Beans
- 2oz of Tomato Paste
- 1 small Zucchini, cut into 1/4-inch-thick slices
- 1 small Green or Red Capsicum, seeded and diced
- Sea Salt to taste
- Freshly ground Black Pepper to taste
- ½ a cup of frozen Green Peas, thawed
- 1 cup of fresh Water

Directions:

1. Blend together the tomato paste, vinegar, garlic, water, ginger, date and coriander along with the other spices until smooth, then set it aside
2. Place the kidney beans, cauliflower, zucchini, capsicum, onions and carrots in your crockpot and stir in the date garlic mixture to combine
3. Cook, covered, on low for 6 hours or 4 hours on high
4. Add the peas and let them to heat through before serving

Nutrition Facts:Per Serving: Cal, 1 total fat 1g, sodium 464mg, carb 32.6g, fiber 10g, protein 9g

Special Olive And Feta Casserole

Servings: 2
Cooking Time: 8 Hours
Ingredients:

- 4 fresh Eggs
- 2 medium sliced boiled Potatoes
- 1 small diced Green Capsicum
- 2oz of finely sliced Portobello Mushrooms
- 2oz of Crumbled Feta
- 2oz of Colby Cheese, shredded
- 2 finely sliced Green Onions
- ¼ of a tsp of White Pepper
- ¼ of a tsp of Sea Salt
- 1 tsp of Olive Oil

Directions:

1. Oil your crockpot
2. Place a single layer of sliced potato in your crockpot
3. Spread a layer each of capsicum, mushrooms, spring onions and cheese on the potatoes. Then another layer of capsicum, mushrooms and green onions
4. Then place in another layer of hash browns, topped with another layer of mushrooms, capsicum and green onions followed by the rest of the cheeses
5. Mix the eggs, salt and pepper together and pour them over the top
6. Cook covered for 4 hours on high or 8 hours on low, then serve with additional sliced spring onions, as a garnish

Nutrition Facts:Per Serving:423 cal, 30g total fat, 398mg chol, 9bsodium, 10.9g carb, 1.1g fiber, 27.7g protein

Homely Healthy Baked Beans

Servings: 2
Cooking Time: 8 Hours
Ingredients:

- 1/2lb of dry Beans, soaked overnight or for 8 hours
- 1 small diced Onion
- 1 diced stalk celery
- 2 cloves of minced Garlic
- ½ a cup of Crushed Tomatoes
- 1 cup of Water
- ¼ of a cup of Olive Oil
- ½ a tbsp of Ground Oregano
- ½ a tbsp of Ground Thyme
- 1 Bay Leaf
- 1 tbsp of Sea Salt

Directions:

1. Place everything in your crockpot and cook, covered, on low for 7-8 hours
2. Serve with feta cheese, fresh baked bread or on toast.

Nutrition Facts:Per Serving: Cal 149, total fat 1.1g, sat fat 0.2g, sodium 751mg, carb .5g, fiber 19.4g protein 12.8g

Amazing Greek Gigantes In Tomato Sauce

Servings: 2
Cooking Time: 8 Hours
Ingredients:
- 1/2lb of dry Gigantes Beans, soaked overnight
- 1 peeled and chopped Onions
- 1 clove of diced Garlic
- ½ a cup of diced Tomatoes
- ¼ of a cup of Sun-dried Tomatoes
- 1 cup of Vegetable Stock
- 1 Bay Leaf
- ½ a tsp of dried Oregano
- ¼ of a tsp, of dried Thyme
- 1 pinch of Red Pepper Flakes
- Sea Salt to taste
- 1 tbsp of Extra Virgin Olive Oil
- Crusty Bread, Black Pepper, and some more Olive Oil for serving

Directions:
1. Place all the ingredients into your crockpot and cook covered for 8 hours on low or 4 hours on high
2. Taste and add salt or pepper if required
3. This dish can be a whole meal or an accompaniment
4. Garnish with freshly ground black pepper and a drizzle of olive oil

Nutrition Facts:Per Serving:182 cal, 9,1g total fat, 1.6g sat fat, 2mg chol, 8 sodium, 23.4g carb 6.8g fiber, 4.7 protein

Italian, Vegan Casserole With Quinoa

Servings:2
Cooking Time: 5 Hours
Ingredients:
- ¾ of a cup of soaked, dried Chickpeas
- 1 medium Potato
- 2 medium Carrots
- 1 small Onion
- 1 cup of cooked Quinoa
- 1 tsp of crushed Red Peppers
- 2 tsp of Paprika
- 1 tbsp of Miso
- 1 tbsp of Tamari or Soy Sauce
- 1 tbsp of Mirin
- 1 tbsp of Pomegranate Molasses
- 1 tbsp of Balsamic Vinegar
- 1 clove of crushed Garlic
- 1 tbsp of Sesame Oil
- 1 sliced Spring Onions
- ¼ of a cup of Toasted Sliced Almonds

Directions:
1. Wash and slice the carrots, onions and potatoes into bite sized pieces
2. Place everything except the quinoa spring onions and sliced almonds in your crockpot and stir to combine
3. Cook, covered, for 6 hours on high
4. Serve the casserole over the cooked quinoa garnished with sliced spring onions and almonds

Nutrition Facts:Per Serving:602 cal, 11.2g total fat, 1.4g sat fat, 770mg sodium, 106g carb, 18.2g fiber, 22.protein

Individual Egg And Vegetable Frittatas

Servings:4
Cooking Time: 5 Hours
Ingredients:
- 1 ⅓ cups corn kernels, frozen
- 1 cup kale, chopped
- 1 cup red bell pepper, chopped
- 1 cup green onion, chopped
- ¼ tbsp dried thyme
- Cooking spray
- 4 eggs
- 4 egg whites
- ¼ tbsp salt
- 1 cup water
- 2 oz cheddar cheese, reduced-fat

Directions:
1. Coat four ramekins with cooking spray and divide the kernels, kale, pepper, and green onions among the ramekins.
2. Pack the veggies by pressing using a spoon back.
3. In a mixing bowl, whisk together eggs, egg whites, salt, and thyme. Carefully pour over each ramekin.
4. Coat a paper foil with cooking spray and cover the ramekins individually.
5. Add water to the crockpot and place a trivet in place. Place the ramekins on the trivet and stack the fourth ramekin on the other ramekins.
6. Set the timer for ten minutes on high. When time elapses, remove lid and remove the ramekins from the crockpot.
7. Remove the foil from the ramekins and sprinkle with more salt and cheese. Let rest for peak flavors.
8. Serve and enjoy.

Nutrition Facts:Per Serving: Calories 200, Total Fat 8g, Saturated Fat 3g, Total Carbs 15g, Net Carbs 11g, Protein 16g, Sugar 5g, Fiber 3g, Sodium 440mg, Potassium 410 mg

Mediterranean Style Beans And Vegetables

Servings: 2
Cooking Time: 8 Hours
Ingredients:
- ½ a cup of Great Northern Beans, drained and rinsed
- ½ a cup of Red Beans, drained and rinsed
- 1 tsp of minced Garlic
- 1 small chopped Onion
- 1 thinly sliced Carrots
- 1 stick of thinly sliced Celery
- 1/2 a cup of cleaned and cut fresh Green Beans
- 1 chopped Red Chili Peppers, or to taste
- 1 tbsp of Tomato Paste
- 1 Bay Leaves
- Sea Salt to taste
- Freshly Cracked Black Pepper, to taste

Directions:
1. Place everything straight into your crockpot and cook covered on the low setting for 8 hours, or until tender. Remove the bay leaf and serve

Nutrition Facts:Per Serving:195.4 cal, 0.8g total fat, 0. sat fat, 25.9 sodium, 37.1g carb, 10.9g fiber, 12.3 protein

Spicy Vegetarian Chili

Servings:2
Cooking Time:4 Hours
Ingredients:
- ½ a cup of Farro
- 1 small diced Onion
- 1 clove of minced garlic
- 1 chopped Chipotle Chili in Adobo Sauce
- ½ a cup of drained Dark Red Kidney Beans
- ½ a cup of drained Light Red Kidney Beans
- ½ a cup of Tomato Sauce
- ½ a cup of Diced Tomatoes
- 2 tbsp of Chopped Green Chiles
- 1 cup of Vegetable Stock
- ½ a cup of Beer or Vegetable Broth
- 1 tsp of Chili Powder
- 1/2 tbsp of Ground Cumin
- Sea Salt to taste
- Freshly Ground Black Pepper to taste

Directions:
1. Place everything in your crockpot and cook, covered, on high for 4 hours or low for 8 hours
2. Taste it and adjust the seasoning
3. Serve garnished with extra toppings if desired

Nutrition Facts:Per Serving:23cal, 2.6g total fat, 0.3g sat fat 687mg sodium, 42.2g carb, 8.8g fiber, 12.4 protein

Delightful Ratatouille

Servings: 2
Cooking Time: 3 Hours
Ingredients:
- 1 small Aubergine (Eggplant) cut into inch cubes
- 1 medium chopped Ripe Tomato
- 1 medium sliced Zucchini (Courgette)
- 1 small chopped Onion
- 1 small chopped Sweet Green Capsicum (Pepper)
- 1 small chopped Sweet Yellow Capsicum (Pepper)
- 1 small chopped Sweet Red Capsicum (Pepper)
- 2 tbsp of pitted Green Olives
- 2 tbsp of pitted Black Olives
- 1 tbsp of Tomato Paste
- 1 tbsp of minced Fresh Basil
- ½ tsp of Cracked Black Pepper
- 2 tsp of Olive Oil

Directions:
1. Place everything in your crockpot and cook covered on high for 4 hours or low for 7 hours

Nutrition Facts:Per Serving: Al 1, total fat 7g, Sat fat 1g, Carbs 15g protein 3g, fiber4g, Sodium 488g

Vegan Thai Mushroom Soup

Servings:4
Cooking Time: 45 Minutes
Ingredients:

- 8 oz Cremini mushrooms, sliced
- 15 oz chickpeas, no added salt
- 1 tbsp sriracha
- ½ tbsp cumin, ground
- 1 ½ cup lite coconut milk
- Pepper and onion blend, frozen
- 14 ½ oz tomatoes, diced
- ½ cup water
- ½ cup cilantro
- 1 tbsp ginger, fresh
- ½ tbsp salt

Directions:

1. Add mushrooms, pepper and onion blend, chickpeas, diced tomatoes, sriracha, cumin, and water in the crockpot.
2. Cover the crockpot and cook for eight minutes on high.
3. When the time elapses, remove the lid and stir in the remaining ingredients.
4. Let rest for five minutes to allow the flavors to blend.
5. Serve and enjoy when warm.

Nutrition Facts:Per Serving: Calories 240, Total Fat 7g, Saturated Fat 5g, Total Carbs 7g, Net Carbs 28g, Protein 12g, Sugar 8g, Fiber 7g, Sodium 440mg, Potassium 930 mg

Hearty Cabbage Soup

Servings:9
Cooking Time: 1 Hour
Ingredients:

- 2 carrots, diced
- 2 celery stalks, diced
- ½ lb. turkey breakfast sausage, lean
- 40 oz chicken broth, low sodium
- 15 ½ Great northern beans
- Cooking spray
- 1 onion, diced
- ½ cabbage chopped
- 14 ½ tomato, diced
- ¼ tbsp black pepper
- ½ tbsp dried oregano

Directions:

1. Spray your crockpot with cooking spray and set to low
2. Add onion, carrots, and celery, and sauté until onions are clear.
3. Remove from pot and set aside. Add turkey sausage to the crockpot and cook on high until browned.
4. Add the onion mixture and mix well. Add all the remaining ingredients and bring to boil.
5. Cover the crockpot and simmer at low for ten minutes.
6. Serve and enjoy.

Nutrition Facts:Per Serving: Calories 120, Total Fat 2.5g, Saturated Fat 1g, Total Carbs 15g, Net Carbs 10g, Protein 10g, Sugar 9g, Fiber 5g, Sodium 360mg, Potassium 550 mg

Easy Black Bean Soup

Servings:8
Cooking Time: 6 Hours
Ingredients:

- 28 oz can tomato, diced and undrained
- 38 oz can black beans, drained and rinsed
- 2 ½ cubes McCormick's vegetable Bouillon
- 2 cups green beans, frozen
- 1 onion, chopped
- 4 garlic cloves, crushed
- 2 tbsp cumin, ground
- 2 tbsp ginger, ground
- 2 tbsp curry powder

Directions:

1. Add all ingredients in your crockpot except the bouillon cubes.
2. Dissolve the bouillon cubes in hot water and add to the crockpot.
3. Add water to your desired level.
4. Set timer for seven hours. When time elapses, put in serving cups; two cups per serving.
5. Enjoy.

Nutrition Facts:Per Serving: Calories 210, Total Fat 1.8g, Saturated Fat 0g, Total Carbs 35g, Net Carbs 28g, Protein 12.2g, Sugar 8g, Fiber 9.2g, Sodium 1323mg, Potassium 980 mg

Dreamy Kale & Cannellini Casserole With Farro

Servings: 2
Cooking Time: 6 Hours
Ingredients:

- 1 cup of Vegetable Stock or Broth
- ½ a cup of Unsalted, Fire-Roasted Tomatoes
- ½ a cup of rinsed Farro
- 1 small coarsely chopped Onion
- 1 thinly sliced medium Carrots
- 1 diced Celery Stalk
- 1 clove of crushed Garlic,
- 1/2 a tsp of crushed Red Pepper
- 1/4 of a tsp of Sea Salt
- 2 cups of coarsely chopped fresh Green Kale
- ½ a cup of Cannellini Beans, rinsed and drained
- 1 tbsp of fresh Lemon Juice
- ¼ of a cup of crumbled Feta Cheese
- A hand full of chopped fresh Basil or Parsley

Directions:

1. Place the farro, stock, tomatoes, onions, celery, carrots, garlic, crushed red pepper, and salt in your crockpot and cook, covered on high for 2 hours
2. Stir in the beans, kale and the lemon juice, then continue cooking, covered for about another hour
3. Serve with a sprinkling of parsley, cheese or fresh basil

Nutrition Facts:Per Serving: Cal 27 fat 4g, chol 11mg, sodium 691mg, carb 46g, fiber 9g, protein 14g

Asian Spaghetti Squash

Servings:6
Cooking Time: 7 Hours
Ingredients:
- 3 lb. spaghetti squash
- 3 tbsp soy sauce, low sodium
- 12 oz shelled edamame, frozen
- 1 cup matchstick carrots
- 1 cup water
- 2 limes
- 4 tbsp sugar
- ⅛ tbsp red pepper flakes, crushed
- 1 tbsp ginger, grated
- ½ cup green onions, chopped
- ½ fresh cilantro, chopped

Directions:
1. Use a knife to pierce the entire surface of the squash. Place the squash in the microwave to cook for two minutes.
2. Remove the squash from the microwave and cut it crosswise. Remove the seeds and the connecting strands.
3. Pour water in the crockpot and place the two squash halves on the trivet. Cover the crockpot and cook for seven minutes.
4. Meanwhile, combine soy sauce, one lime juice, sugar, pepper, and ginger in a mixing bowl. Mix until well incorporated.
5. When the time is done, remove the squash from the crockpot and place it on a cutting board.
6. Add the shelled edamame to the cooking liquid and bring it to boil. Let it boil for two minutes then drain well.
7. Run a fork around the squash outer edges to release spaghetti squash strands.
8. Divide the squash among six bowls and top with edamame, soy sauce mixture, carrots, onions, and sprinkle with cilantro.
9. Cut the remaining limes into six equal pieces and place them on each bowl.
10. Serve and enjoy.

Nutrition Facts:Per Serving: Calories 180, Total Fat 8g, Saturated Fat 0.5g, Total Carbs 21g, Net Carbs 15g, Protein 10g, Sugar 9g, Fiber 6g, Sodium 320mg, Potassium 820 mg

Garlic, Herb And Mushroom Surprise

Servings: 2
Cooking Time: 4 Hours
Ingredients:
- 12oz of Cremini Mushrooms
- 2 cloves of minced Garlic
- 2 small mild Green Chilies
- 2 small mild Red Chillies
- ¼ of a tsp of dried Basil
- ¼ of a tsp of dried Oregano
- ¼ of a tsp of dried thyme
- 1 Bay Leaf
- ½ a cup of Vegetable Stock
- 1 tbsp of Unsalted Butter
- 1 tbsp of chopped fresh Parsley

Directions:
1. Place everything except the butter in your crockpot and cook covered on low for 4 hours
2. During the last 15 minutes of Cooking time: stir in the butter, then serve with parsley

Nutrition Facts:Per Serving: Cal 120, total fat 8g, sat fat 4.5g, Chol 20mg, Sodium 450mg, carb 9g, fiber 2g, protein 6g

Amazing Vegetable Lasagna

Servings: 2
Cooking Time: 4 Hours
Ingredients:
- 3oz of baby Spinach, chopped and drained
- 1 clove of minced Garlic
- 1 tbsp of minced fresh Oregano
- ½ a cup of diced Tomatoes
- ½ a cup of Marinara Sauce
- ½ a box of Lasagna Noodles
- 6oz of Ricotta Cheese
- 1 cup of Mozzarella Cheese
- 2 tbsp of Parmesan Cheese
- ¼ of a tsp of Black Pepper
- ¼ of a tsp of Red Pepper Flakes

Directions:
1. Combine the ricotta, Parmesan, pepper, pepper flakes, garlic, oregano in one bowl
2. Combine the diced tomatoes. Marinara sauce and parsley in another bowl
3. Place a little sauce mixture on the bottom of your crockpot
4. Add a layer of noodles and half of the baby spinach
5. Add a third of the ricotta mixture and a third of the mozzarella
6. Then a layer of the tomato sauce
7. Add a layer of noodles and repeat finishing with the last of the cheeses on top

Nutrition Facts:Per Serving: Cal, 350, Total fat19g, Sat fat 10g, Chol 55mg, Sodium omg, Carb 29g, fiber 6g Protein 19g

Coconut Quinoa Curry

Servings: 2
Cooking Time: 4 Hours
Ingredients:
- 1 cup of chopped Sweet Potato
- 1 cup of Broccoli Florets
- 1 small chopped Onion
- ½ a cup of drained and rinsed Chickpeas
- ½ a cup of diced Tomatoes
- 1 cup of Coconut Milk
- ¼ of a cup of Quinoa
- 1 clove of minced Garlic
- ½ a tbsp of minced Ginger
- 1 tsp of grated Turmeric
- 1 tsp of Tamari Sauc1/4 of a tsp of chili Flakes

Directions:
1. Place everything in your crockpot and stir the cook covered for 4 hours on high and serve when the sweet potatoes are tender

Nutrition Facts:Per Serving: Cal 507, Total Fat 3, Sat fat 26g, Sodium 380mg, Carb 50g, fiber 11g, protein 13g

Heavenly Vegan White Bean Stew

Servings:2
Cooking Time: 10 Hours

Ingredients:

- 1/2lb of White Beans
- 1 small diced Carrot
- 1 small Celery Stalk
- 1 small diced Onion
- 1 clove of minced Garlic
- 1 Bay Leaf
- ½ a tsp of dried Rosemary
- ½ a tsp of dried Thyme
- ½ a tsp of dried Oregano
- 3 to 6 cups of Fresh Drinking Water
- 1 tbsp of Sea Salt, more or less to taste
- Freshly ground White Pepper, to taste
- ½ a cup of Diced Tomatoes
- 2 or 3 cups (or more) of Green Leafy Green Vegetables (kale, chard, spinach) roughly chopped
- Couscous, polenta for serving

Directions:

1. Place the soaked beans in your crockpot, covered with the water
2. Cook, covered, for 8 to 10 hours on low
3. Then add the carrots, onion, celery, garlic, bay leaf, and dried herbs
4. Cook, covered, on low for to 7
5. When the beans are tender, add the tomatoes, salt and pepper to taste
6. Add the greens about 15 minutes before serving
7. They can be served hot, warm or cold over couscous, polenta or bread

Nutrition Facts:Per Serving:336, cal, 0.9g Total fat, 0.2g sat fat, 136mg sodium, 65.7g carb, 16.4g fiber, 233 g protein

Exotic Curried Vegetable And Chickpea Casserole

Servings: 2
Cooking Time: 8 Hours

Ingredients:

- ½ a cup of Cauliflower, cut into bite-sized florets
- 1 small diced Onion
- 1 small diced Green Capsicum
- 1 small diced Red Capsicum
- 1 small diced Potato
- 2.5oz of Baby Spinach
- 1 tsp of grated fresh Ginger
- 1 clove of minced Garlic
- 1 cup of low-sodium Vegetable stock
- ½ a cup of drained and rinsed Chickpeas
- 1/2 a cup of diced Tomatoes with the juices
- ½ a cup of Coconut Milk
- 1 tsp of Curry Powder more or less to taste
- A dash of Cayenne Pepper or to taste
- 1 tbsp of Sea Salt, divided
- 1/4 of a tsp of freshly ground Black Pepper

Directions:

1. Place everything except the spinach and coconut milk in your crockpot and stir it to mix thoroughly
2. Cook, covered, on high for 4 hours
3. Then stir in the coconut milk
4. Add the spinach and let it wilt in the residual heat
5. Check and adjust the seasoning if necessary
6. Serve over couscous or orzo pasta

Nutrition Facts:Per Serving: Cal 261, total fat 5.1g, sat fat 1g, carb 44.6g, fiber 11.5g, chol 13.1mg, sodium 9.9mg, protein 12.5g

Other Favorite Recipes

Sweet Potato Mash

Servings: 4
Cooking Time: 5 Hours
Ingredients:
- 2 lbs. sweet potatoes, peel & cut in ½-inch slices
- 1 cup apple juice, unsweetened
- 1 tbsp. cinnamon
- 1 ½ tsp nutmeg
- 1 tsp allspice
- ½ tsp cloves

Directions:
1. Place the sweet potatoes and ½ cup juice in the crock pot. Add half the spices and mix.
2. Add the lid and cook on low heat 4-5 hours or until potatoes are tender.
3. Use an immersion blender to process potatoes, adding the other half of the juice and spices, until the mixture is almost smooth. serve.

Nutrition Facts:Per Serving: Calories 1, total Carbs 28g, net Carbs 24g, Fiber 4g, Protein 2g, Fat 3g, saturated Fat 0g, sugar 8g, sodium 64mg, Cholesterol 0mg

Southern Green Beans

Servings: 16
Cooking Time: 8 Hours
Ingredients:
- 2 tbsp. extra virgin olive oil
- 1 onion, diced
- 2 cloves garlic, diced fine
- 1 tbsp. fresh basil, chopped
- 1 tsp pepper
- 2 lbs. fresh snap green beans, rinsed & strings removed
- 1 potato, peeled & diced
- 3 cups vegetable broth, low-sodium
- ½ tsp salt

Directions:
1. Heat oil in a skillet over med-low heat.
2. Add onion and garlic and cook until soft, about 4 minutes. transfer to crock pot.
3. Add remaining ingredients and stir to mix.
4. Add the lid and cook on low heat 8 hours or until beans are fork-tender.

Nutrition Facts:Per Serving: Calories 37, total Carbs 6g, net Carbs 4g, Fiber 2g, Protein 2g, Fat 1g, saturated Fat 0g, sugar 1g, sodium 101mg, Cholesterol 0mg

Caulimac & Cheese

Servings: 6
Cooking Time: 4 Hours
Ingredients:

- nonstick cooking spray
- 1 head cauliflower, separated into small florets
- ½ cup onion, chopped
- ¼ tsp salt
- ¼ tsp black pepper
- 2 tbsp. butter, divided
- 2 tbsp. whole wheat flour
- 1 cup skim milk
- 1 tsp yellow mustard
- ½ tsp garlic powder
- 1 ½ cup sharp cheddar cheese, reduced-fat, grated
- 2 tbsp. whole wheat bread crumbs

Directions:

1. spray crock pot with cooking spray.
2. Place cauliflower and onion in the crock pot. Add salt and pepper and toss to combine.
3. Melt 1 ½ tablespoons butter in a medium saucepan over medium heat.
4. Whisk in flour. Add milk and whisk until sauce thickens.
5. stir in mustard, garlic powder, and cheese and cook, stirring until mixture is smooth. Pour over cauliflower and mix well.
6. Melt remaining butter in a small saucepan over medium heat. stir in bread crumbs. sprinkle over cauliflower mixture.
7. Add lid and cook on low heat 4 hours, or until cauliflower is tender and the mixture is hot and bubbly. serve.

Nutrition Facts:Per Serving: Calories 177, total Carbs 9g, net Carbs 7g, Fiber 2g, Protein 11g, Fat 11g, saturated Fat 5g, sugar 4g, sodium 370mg, Cholesterol 22mg

Butternut Risotto

Servings: 12
Cooking Time: 90 Minutes
Ingredients:

- 1 tbsp. olive oil
- ½ cup onion, chopped
- 2 cloves garlic, diced fine
- 1 cup Arborio rice, uncooked
- 2 cups butternut squash, cubed
- 2 ½ cups vegetable broth, low sodium
- ½ tsp cinnamon
- ¼ tsp salt
- ¼ tsp pepper

Directions:

1. Heat oil in a large skillet over medium heat.
2. Add onion and garlic and cook until translucent, about 3-4 minutes.
3. Add rice and cook, occasionally stirring, minutes. transfer to the crock pot.
4. Add remaining ingredients and stir to mix.
5. Add lid and cook on high 90 minutes, or until rice is soft. stir before serving.

Nutrition Facts:Per Serving: Calories 90, total Carbs 17g, net Carbs 1, Fiber 1g, Protein 2g, Fat 1g, saturated Fat 0g, sugar 1g, sodium 65mg, Cholesterol 0mg

Cauliflower Fried "rice"

Servings: 8
Cooking Time: 4 Hours
Ingredients:

- 2 heads cauliflower, grated
- 1 tbsp. fresh ginger, grated
- 1 tbsp. garlic, diced fine
- ½ cup vegetable broth, low sodium
- 2 eggs
- 1 cup mixed vegetables, frozen
- ¼ cup green onions, diced
- ¼ cup cilantro, chopped
- 2 tbsp. soy sauce, low sodium

Directions:

1. Combine cauliflower, ginger, garlic, and broth in the crock pot.
2. Add the lid and cook on low heat 3-4 hours, or on high hours.
3. In a medium bowl, whisk the eggs.
4. Heat 1 teaspoon butter in a skillet over medium heat. Add eggs and scramble.
5. When the cauliflower is tender, add scrambled eggs and vegetables. Continue cooking 30 minutes or until vegetables are heated through.
6. stir in green onions and cilantro. drizzle with soy sauce and serve.

Nutrition Facts:Per Serving: Calories 86, total Carbs 11g, net Carbs , Fiber 4g, Protein 7g, Fat 2g, saturated Fat 1g, sugar 3g, sodium 201mg, Cholesterol 46mg

28-Day Meal Plan

Day 1
Breakfast: Shrimp & Broccoli Breakfast Casserole
Lunch: Super Tasty Tex-mex Chicken
Dinner: Seafood Stew
Day 2
Breakfast: Cool Breakfast Burritos
Lunch: Exquisite Stuffed Squid
Dinner: Tilapia Stew With Green Peppers
Day 3
Breakfast: Amazing Overnight Apple And Cinnamon Oatmeal
Lunch: Chicken Mushroom Stew
Dinner: Delicious Tuna Mornay
Day 4
Breakfast: Mouth Watering Egg Casserole
Lunch: Turkey Sausage & Barley Soup
Dinner: Magical Coconut Cilantro Currie Shrimp
Day 5
Breakfast: Dreamy Lemon Berry Steel Cut Oats
Lunch: Rich Crab, Spinach And Egg Casserole
Dinner: Heavenly Vegan White Bean Stew
Day 6
Breakfast: Delicious Apple Blueberry Risotto
Lunch: Cheesy Chicken Broccoli Casserole
Dinner: Heavenly Seafood Chowder
Day 7
Breakfast: Delectable Potato Bake
Lunch: African Beef Stew
Dinner: Magic Whole Stuffed Squash
Day 8
Breakfast: Wonderful Spicy Breakfast Casserole
Lunch: Taco Casserole
Dinner: Fabulous Vindaloo Vegetables
Day 9
Breakfast: Flavorful Greek Egg Casserole
Lunch: Royal Lobster Tails
Dinner: Seafood Gumbo Stock
Day 10
Breakfast: Cauliflower Oatmeal
Lunch: Pork Stew
Dinner: Special Olive And Feta Casserole
Day 11
Breakfast: Crockpot Breakfast Casserole
Lunch: Supreme Salmon
Dinner: Lamb And Lentil Shepherd's Pie
Day 12
Breakfast: Apple Pecan Breakfast Pudding
Lunch: Tender Sunday Roast Beef
Dinner: Homely Healthy Baked Beans
Day 13
Breakfast: Tantalizing Cranberry Apple French Toast
Lunch: Beef Provenca
Dinner: White Beans & Bacon
Day 14
Breakfast: Tomato & Mozzarella Crustless Quiche
Lunch: Healthy Hamburger Casserole
Dinner: Amazing Greek Gigantes In Tomato Sauce
Day 15
Breakfast: Apple & Pumpkin Oatmeal

Lunch: Italian Meatloaf
Dinner: Simple Steamed Crab Legs
Day 16
Breakfast: Savory Oatmeal
Lunch: Sassy Pot Roast
Dinner: Homemade Pork & Beans
Day 17
Breakfast: Berry French Toast Casserole
Lunch: Bbq Pork Chops & Peppers
Dinner: Italian, Vegan Casserole With Quinoa
Day 18
Breakfast: Mouth-watering Egg Casserole
Lunch: Shredded Green Chili Beef
Dinner: Individual Egg And Vegetable Frittatas
Day 19
Breakfast: Peanut Butter & Banana Oatmeal Bars
Lunch: Mexican Meatloaf
Dinner: Flank Steak Tacos
Day 20
Breakfast: Bacon & Tomato Grits
Lunch: Beef Salsa With Squash Noodles And Tomatoes
Dinner: Mediterranean Style Beans And Vegetables
Day 21
Breakfast: Amazing Carrot Cake
Lunch: Pork And Pumpkin Stew
Dinner: Delightful Ratatouille
Day 22
Breakfast: Skinny Pecan Pie
Lunch: Burgundy Braised Lamb Shanks
Dinner: Succulent Pork Chops And Beans
Day 23
Breakfast: Delightful Peach Cobbler
Lunch: African Beef Stew
Dinner: Vegan Thai Mushroom Soup
Day 24
Breakfast: Mozzarella Stuffed Meatballs
Lunch: Balsamic Brisket With Caramelized Onions
Dinner: Hearty Cabbage Soup
Day 25
Breakfast: Meatloaf On A Sling
Lunch: Succulent Salmon With Caramelized Onions
Dinner: Beef And Tomato Lasagna
Day 26
Breakfast: Chocolate Chip Scones
Lunch: Cajun Shrimp Chowder
Dinner: Kielbasa (polish Sausage) With Cabbage And Potatoes
Day 27
Breakfast: No Peel Crockpot Hard-boiled Eggs
Lunch: Pork Pot Roast With Tangerines
Dinner: Easy Black Bean Soup
Day 28
Breakfast: Glazed Tropical Cookie Bars
Lunch: Lamb And Aubergine Casserole
Dinner: Amazing Vegetable Lasagna

Appendix : Recipes Index